choosing
and growing
bonsai

hamlyn

peter chan

choosing
and growing
bonsai

First published in Great Britain in 2007
by Hamlyn, a division of Octopus Publishing
Group Ltd, 2–4 Heron Quays, London E14 4JP

Distributed in the United States and Canada by
Sterling Publishing Co., Inc., 387 Park Avenue
South, New York, NY 10016–8810

ISBN-13: 978-0-600-61442-5
ISBN-10: 0-600-61442-5

A CIP catalogue record for this book
is available from the British Library

Printed and bound in China

10 9 8 7 6 5 4 3 2 1

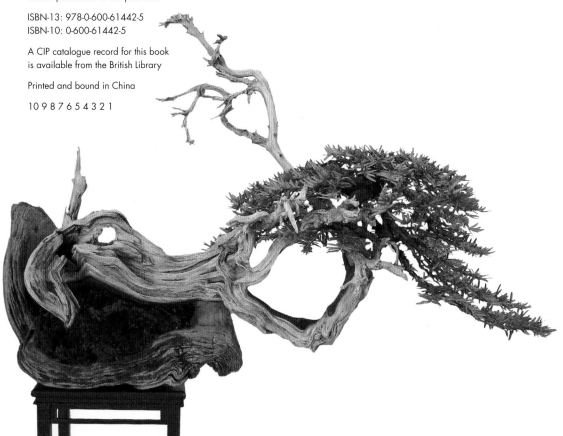

contents

Introduction

Bonsai are now part of our lives. Like oriental food, they are now taken for granted and most people are familiar with them. No longer are these tiny trees regarded as curiosities or botanical freaks as they were a few decades ago. There was a time when they were available only at specialist centres, but now it is possible to buy bonsai in shopping malls and on the internet. They can be found at garden centres and seen at horticultural shows.

Some bonsai are inexpensive, while others can cost a small fortune. As with any commodity, the different styles and grades of bonsai are reflected in the price. You can buy a young, newly trained bonsai with very limited funds, or you can spend thousands on an exquisite masterpiece that has been shown at major exhibitions in Japan. Serious enthusiasts regard good-quality bonsai as works of art and these are highly collectable items.

Although the art of bonsai is essentially about growing trees, for many people it is much more than that. Bonsai say something about the owner's lifestyle, aesthetic sense and attitude towards nature and the environment. Growing bonsai has come to be associated with Zen aesthetics, and some practitioners derive a special therapeutic benefit which comes from the innate peace and tranquillity that working with bonsai imparts. Like yoga and tai chi, bonsai are said to have a calming influence on the mind and spirit, and they can help to relieve the stresses of today's busy world.

Bonsai are certainly beautiful to look at, but there is much more to the pastime than simply achieving beauty. The image of an ancient tree clinging to a rock and struggling to survive against all the odds has been a source of inspiration for Chinese sages and scholars for at least two millennia.

Keeping bonsai is not just about gardening — art and spirituality combine with horticultural techniques. Creating bonsai is a challenge, and enthusiasts are

Left: Juniperus communis is ideal for training in the driftwood style.

Above: Nothing could be more stunning than a Satsuki azalea bonsai in bloom. There are hundreds of varieties in a wide range of colours.

Above: The trailing racemes of wisteria bonsai have a delicious scent.

forever striving for horticultural and aesthetic excellence. Unlike other artistic projects, however, a bonsai is never finished. It continues to grow and change, which means that perfection is always transitory and beauty is only momentary. Growing bonsai is a never-ending quest for perfection. Those who are dedicated to the hobby regard it as a way of life. It requires commitment and can dictate the way you spend your time and resources. Your weekends and holidays can soon become geared around your bonsai activities. Nevertheless, the rewards that come from striving for a perfect work of art more than compensate for the time and effort involved.

Above: In midsummer, stewartia bonsai produce delicate, cup-shaped flowers which resemble those of their near relations, the camellias.

all about
about
bonsai

What is a bonsai?

Most people are familiar with a bonsai's appearance, but what exactly is a bonsai? Not every tree grown in a pot will qualify as a bonsai. For a tree to be regarded as a bonsai, it must have certain defining characteristics: it must be grown in a container, it must have a distinctive artistic shape and it must be miniature in size. A bonsai should be a small-scale replica in a pot of a fully grown tree that you might see in nature, its size and aesthetic appearance controlled by regular pruning, pinching and shaping, watering and feeding.

The 21 styles

The Chinese, who invented bonsai, still refer to them as artistic pot plants, which implies that bonsai are not simply plants in pots but also works of art. To qualify as a bonsai, a tree should conform to one of the distinctive bonsai styles. There are 21 principal shapes, which may be single-trunk, multi-trunk or multi-tree styles.

Left: This trident maple is an excellent specimen, with a fine root buttress and tapered trunk and a natural appearance.

The different formations range from the absolutely straight formal upright style and the S-shaped informal upright style (the most common of bonsai shapes) to the stripped-bark driftwood style, reminiscent of weathered mountain trees, and the broom style, which resembles a domed mop head and is the most natural looking of the styles. For more on shaping your bonsai tree, see pages 194–197.

Chinese beginnings

The art of bonsai has a rich and colourful history. It was the ancient Chinese who first practised the art more than two millennia ago. The word 'bonsai' derives from two Chinese words meaning a potted tree: *bon* (or *poon*) means pot and *sai* (or *sue*) means tree.

The Chinese have been growing ornamental plants for thousands of years – they were one of the earliest civilizations to do so. They also have a tradition for making fine ceramics, which dates back many thousands of years. It is not surprising that when these two arts were brought together the result was bonsai – plants grown in ceramic pots.

The Chinese loved the art of bonsai, but during the 1950s and until the 1980s it was nearly extinguished by the communist regime, which regarded growing bonsai as a revisionist and bourgeois pastime. It is only in

Above: These Chinese elms make a good example of Chinese bonsai style. They have been planted in the landscape or *pen-jing* style.

Above: This trident maple has been trained in the Japanese style, which is usually less ornamental than the Chinese approach.

the last few decades that the Chinese authorities have started to encourage the practice of bonsai again, and now it is once more a thriving and vibrant art form. For some people it is a pleasant and enthralling way to pass the time, but for others it is big business, and almost all the indoor bonsai sold around the world today come from China.

The Japanese style

The Japanese are also involved in bonsai, but contrary to popular belief, the practice did not originate in that country. The Japanese started creating bonsai around the 12th century CE, almost a millennium after the Chinese first practised the art. Chinese influences on Japan have been all pervasive. The Japanese language itself, the Buddhist religion and art in general all have their origins in China. Zen Buddhism in particular, which has been such a key influence on Japanese culture, was introduced from China. Similarly, the arts of garden making and bonsai were imported from China. Although Japanese bonsai today are quite different from Chinese examples, it was not until the early 20th century that a distinctive Japanese style of bonsai began to emerge. Up to that time, Chinese and Japanese bonsai were indistinguishable.

Left: This driftwood yew is a good example of the emerging European style of bonsai.

Bonsai today

During the period following World War II, while China was in turmoil, the Japanese began to develop bonsai in their own inimitable style. The US occupying forces in Japan and the Japanese immigrant community in the USA first made bonsai more widely known in the West, and during the second half of the 20th century, the interest in bonsai mushroomed.

Today, there is no corner of the world where bonsai are not grown. They have become established in most Asian countries, including India, Indonesia, Vietnam and Sri Lanka. They have also become popular throughout Europe and North America, and they are grown in Australia, Africa and South America. There is hardly a country today where the art of bonsai is not practised.

As a result of the burgeoning interest in bonsai, each country and each culture has put its own imprint on the hobby. There is undoubtedly a unique Japanese style of bonsai and a unique Chinese style, but there are now also distinct European and North American styles. Each nation has interpreted the art of bonsai in its own way and put its imprint on the tradition. Each culture has learned to express its own identity through the beauty of these miniature trees. This is why keeping bonsai is such a fascinating art.

Above: Even the humble fuchsia can be made into a bonsai. It is the shaping that makes the difference between an ordinary shrub and an artistic pot plant.

Above: The autumn tints of *Acer palmatum* species are stunning.

Above: New candles emerging on a *Pinus parviflora* bonsai.

Getting started

There are many ways of starting to keep bonsai, but the easiest is to buy a plant from a reputable nursery or specialist bonsai centre. However, before you do so, do a little research and find out more about bonsai. Buying on impulse is not a good idea, especially if your first purchase is from a non-specialist centre such as a shopping mall or market stall. Buying on the internet can also be something of a hit and miss affair. Joining a bonsai or gardening club, if there is one in your neighbourhood, is a good way to start and will be an invaluable source of advice about where and what to buy.

What is involved?

Watering is by far the most important task because bonsai are always grown in containers (often shallow ones) and so depend entirely on their owner for their water supply. In summer, your bonsai will need to be watered once or sometimes twice a day. Even in winter, when there is normally an ample supply of natural rain, bonsai that are kept outside require watering during dry spells, while indoor bonsai will need water all year round. Bonsai keeping is therefore quite a time-consuming pastime, and you will need to be prepared to make the commitment to watering on a regular basis if you want to keep your trees alive.

Above: Special pots, like these handmade ones, are an integral part of bonsai. After all, a bonsai is by definition a tree in a pot.

You won't be able to go away on holiday without making arrangements for the care of your bonsai. Some enthusiasts take their trees to a bonsai nursery, others arrange for bonsai 'sitters' or 'minders' to look after their bonsai while they are away. Fortunately,

the development of automatic irrigation systems has made both holiday and general watering care much easier, and installing a reliable computerized system will allow you to go away for a fortnight without having to worry about your trees.

However, there are also other chores. Most importantly, pruning and pinching new shoots has to be done during the growing season. If your plants are vigorous growers, this can be a time-consuming task. (For more details on bonsai care, see pages 194–205.)

Above: A display of accent or companion plants, used in bonsai displays, at an exhibition in Britain. Bonsai exhibitions are now quite common throughout the world.

Space

Space is another factor to think about before you make your first purchase. Although bonsai may be small in size, a collection of just a few trees can soon take up all the available space in your garden. Many enthusiasts like to display their trees in authentic oriental garden settings, and this involves constructing suitable display areas to show off the trees. When this is done well, the bonsai look stunning. However, you would have to dedicate a large part of your garden to this type of arrangement – and that might not accord with the way the rest of your family would like to use the garden!

Keeping indoor bonsai also requires some planning, because each tree needs to be placed in the best possible location for its particular requirements. Sunny windowsills and special growing areas are not always available, so consider carefully before you buy a large indoor bonsai.

Starting from scratch

If you are a beginner thinking about obtaining your first bonsai, avoid attempting to grow a tree from seeds or cuttings. It is perfectly possible to grow bonsai this way (see pages 202–203), but for a bonsai novice it will be an unnecessarily long and, sometimes, tedious process. There are much

easier ways of getting started – go to a good bonsai nursery and choose a ready-made plant.

Exhibitions and competitions

Visiting exhibitions is one of the best ways to see top-quality bonsai. You will derive inspiration from the plants on display, and as you get drawn into the hobby you might want to exhibit your own plants and enter competitions. Dedicated exhibitions are quite common wherever bonsai are popular – in many European, Asian and American countries, as well as in Japan and China. The Kokofu Ten (*ten* means 'exhibition' in Japanese) is perhaps the most prestigious event. It is held in the first week of February each year in Tokyo, and 300 of the best bonsai in Japan are put on show. The national bonsai organizations will be able to give you more information about such events.

In the West, many flower and horticultural shows have a section devoted to bonsai, and many nurseries and bonsai clubs put on splendid displays. If you have some good bonsai and want to exhibit them, the best way forward is to join your local bonsai club. Many clubs stage bonsai exhibitions that are open to the public, and many of these exhibitions are competitive, as this is seen as a way of raising the standard of the displays.

Choosing and buying bonsai

Most people buy their first bonsai because they think it is attractive or will suit their decor. But this is not a good basis on which to make your choice. If you are a beginner, you should select a species that is easy to keep and that is appropriate for the conditions you are able to offer. If you have a sunny garden or a living room that is bathed in sunlight every afternoon, look for species that will appreciate the environment and avoid shade-loving plants, which will not thrive in direct sun. If your garden is near the sea, consider the problem of salt-laden winds, which can damage delicate foliage.

Selecting your first plant

The health and vigour of the tree should be prime considerations. Never buy a bonsai that looks sick, even if it is being offered at a knock-down price. If there is something wrong with it, the chances are that it may not recover, and when it dies you will have wasted your money. A healthy tree will look fresh, and the leaves will be turgid and well coloured. Avoid plants with limp or shrivelled foliage.

If you are buying in spring or summer, the leaves should be green and cover the branches well. In autumn and winter they will look less fresh, and deciduous trees will be changing colour before the leaves fall in autumn. Judging the health of a deciduous plant in winter can be difficult, because it will have shed all its leaves.

As well as the health and vigour of the tree, you should evaluate the physical characteristics. Look for a good trunk which tapers gradually from a broad base to narrow apex, and clearly visible surface roots which radiate evenly from the trunk base. You should also look for an elegant placement and arrangement of branches, and a fine branch ramification. These factors may not matter much if the tree you are buying is cheap, but must be taken into consideration if you are thinking about investing in an expensive bonsai. Two trees of a similar size can vary enormously in price, depending on whether they possess the qualities prized by enthusiasts. If possible, try to take someone who has experience of growing bonsai with you when choosing an expensive plant.

Above: In a good bonsai nursery, you will be able to find bonsai of every species, shape, size, style and price.

Pricing bonsai

How much you have to pay for your bonsai will depend on several factors, including where you live; whether the bonsai is an indoor or outdoor type; the bonsai's country of origin; the species or variety; the size of the bonsai; the age of the bonsai; and, as discussed above, its overall quality.

Where you live: If you live in China or Japan, where bonsai are grown commercially in vast numbers, you will obviously pay less for your tree. When trees are exported to the West, the price is raised by all the overheads and profit margins involved in the export process.

Type of tree: Indoor bonsai tend to be less expensive than the outdoor (hardy) trees because most come from China, where production costs are low. The imported outdoor trees often come from Japan, where production costs are higher. In addition, indoor trees are intended for the mass market and tend to be of poorer quality, and therefore cheaper, than the outdoor examples from Japan.

Country of origin: Only two countries, Japan and China, have a sizeable export trade in bonsai. They are grown commercially in Korea and Taiwan, but on a lesser scale. Chinese bonsai are much cheaper than Japanese bonsai for

Above: When buying bonsai, look for features such as visible surface roots.

Above: Ugly roots and bad trunk scarring reduce the value of this bonsai.

Above: Buy bonsai that appear to be healthy. If you are buying a pine, the needles should be plump and a fresh green in colour.

Above: The author in front of a very large bonsai at the Shanghai Botanic Garden. The gardeners are giving the tree its autumn trim.

Above: Bonsai come in all shapes and sizes. This is a *mame* or miniature cherry tree. The pot is about the size of a thimble.

two main reasons: their production costs are lower, and they produce mainly fast-growing, tropical indoor varieties. Japanese trees tend to be of much higher quality, and they are, on the whole, the ones that most bonsai enthusiasts in the West prefer.

Species: As with all things, there are fashions in bonsai. What was popular ten or twenty years ago is not popular now. There was a time when *Picea jezoensis* (Yezo spruce) and *Juniperus rigida* (needle juniper) were popular species. Now you are more likely to see *Juniperus chinensis* (Chinese juniper). Similarly, Satsuki azaleas enjoyed a huge vogue about twenty years ago, but now they are less popular. Prices reflect what is in demand.

Size: Bonsai may be miniature trees, but they come in a huge range of sizes. The most common are bonsai that can be carried easily in one hand. Next in popularity are the bonsai that can be carried in two hands. Then there are trees that are 1 m (3 ft) or more high and need two people to lift and move them. There are even some examples that can only be moved by several people. At the other end of the scale are the bonsai that are grown in thimble-size pots. The Japanese have names for all the different sizes, and bonsai exhibitions and competitions have strict criteria for judging the various categories. However, the amateur grower is less likely to be concerned with the different size categories than with the overall beauty of the tree.

As a rule, the larger the bonsai, the more expensive it will be. This is because the taller trees take longer to grow, require bigger, more expensive pots and cost more to transport. But size isn't everything, of course, and a top-quality small bonsai can cost more than a larger but poorer example of the same species.

Age: As with size, age is also important in determining the price of a bonsai, and an older bonsai will be more expensive than a similar, younger example. Ultimately, however, the beauty of the plant is the overriding factor.

Where to buy

The best place to buy bonsai and bonsai accessories is a specialist bonsai nursery. Finding sources should not be difficult if you have access to the internet, but take care before you buy, as many so-called 'specialists' encountered online are not specialists at all. They are middle men who have little or no knowledge of bonsai, and simply buy and sell bonsai items from their homes. If you are making your first serious purchase, try to get a second opinion about potential sources from a local bonsai club or horticultural society. Some large garden centres stock a good range of bonsai and may even have a resident expert to give you advice.

Department stores, shopping malls and hardware stores are not the ideal places to buy bonsai. They do not offer the bonsai an ideal living environment, and trees sold from these outlets are rarely in good condition. The staff are also unlikely to know anything about growing and caring for bonsai.

If you want to buy on the internet, make sure the firm is a reputable one. Download details of the address and telephone number, so that you can get in touch with the supplier if there are any problems. A specialist nursery, which gives personal advice, is always best, especially if you need aftercare service.

Above: A very old driftwood Chinese juniper bonsai. The age of the tree and the popularity of the style make it very valuable.

Indoor and outdoor bonsai

A common misconception about bonsai is that they have to be grown indoors. Many people regard them as delicate, fragile plants, which need to be protected from the elements. They tend to forget that bonsai are trees and that their natural environment is in the open. There are, of course, some types of bonsai that can be grown indoors, but these are often tropical plants, which would not survive if they were grown outdoors in temperate climates. It is important to distinguish between indoor and outdoor bonsai because the two types require different growing conditions and care regimes.

The 'real' bonsai?

Bonsai growers often regard the outdoor plants as the 'real' bonsai. These are the trees and shrubs that will grow outside without special protection. Many bonsai enthusiasts grow only outdoor bonsai because they are much easier to care for and there is more scope for creativity – as outdoor bonsai grow faster than indoor bonsai, you will see the results of reshaping, wiring and pruning much sooner.

This is not to say that outdoor bonsai cannot be taken indoors from time to time. In fact, in countries such as China and Japan, it is traditional to use bonsai to decorate the home, but the trees are kept indoors for only short periods. After a day or two they are returned to their outdoor positions. It may be this tradition

Right: Bougainvillea must be grown indoors in temperate regions, but make fine outdoor plants in tropical countries.

that initially led Westerners to believe that bonsai should be kept indoors permanently.

As outdoor bonsai are easier to keep, it may be better to avoid selecting an indoor bonsai as your first tree. However, if you live in a flat without a garden, and have no alternative but to keep indoor trees, choose a species that is easy to keep in the conditions you can offer. Genera such as *Ficus* (fig) and some species of *Ulmus* (elm) are easy indoor trees. Once

you have gained experience looking after an easier indoor bonsai for a few months, you can progress to more difficult species.

Indoor bonsai

The advantages of keeping indoor bonsai include the fact that many beginners like to keep their bonsai where they can be seen at all times, and this is one of the main reasons people choose indoor species. They are also useful for decorating a room, reflecting your

Above: Figs, such as this *Ficus microcarpa* 'Green Island', are among the easiest indoor bonsai to care for and will thrive in an indoor environment.

all about bonsai

What's the difference?

Most indoor bonsai are broadleaved tropical and semi-tropical trees. Like *Ficus* (fig), many are also grown as houseplants, so are fairly easy to recognize. A few indoor species, such as *Podocarpus* and *Juniperus procumbens*, are coniferous and could be confused with hardy outdoor bonsai. Outdoor bonsai, on the other hand, are hardy species that grow naturally outside. Broadleaved species, such as *Acer* (maple) and *Crataegus* (hawthorn), and conifers such as *Pinus* (pine) and *Juniperus* (juniper), are not difficult to identify as outdoor plants.

taste and lifestyle. In recent years bonsai have become popular because they are associated with Zen and minimalist styles of decor. Keeping a bonsai makes a statement about your lifestyle.

The main drawback of indoor bonsai is that they are difficult to keep and may not be long lived if you do not provide the appropriate conditions. They need to be watered and fed regularly, and misted from time to time to provide a humid environment. They are also extremely demanding about the ambient temperature, which

must be constant. If you go away for a fortnight's holiday or even a long weekend you will need someone to look after your trees in your absence. Indoor bonsai are, in fact, like demanding pets.

Outdoor bonsai

Outdoor bonsai are far easier to care for, although you will still have to make arrangements for someone to look after them while you are away on holiday.

The choice of outdoor bonsai is much wider than of indoor species. They tend to be more attractive

than indoor trees, especially the deciduous and flowering subjects. Because they are easier to keep, outdoor bonsai live longer than indoor specimens. Indeed, some outdoor bonsai can live for more than a hundred years.

Outdoor bonsai also offer more scope for practising the hobby. Some enthusiasts make their own bonsai from garden and nursery plants, and some collect the raw material from the wild. You can also propagate your own plants from seed or cuttings or by layering (see pages 202–203).

outdoor
coniferous
bonsai

Outdoor coniferous bonsai

Nearly all the conifers are evergreen, and evergreen trees have always had a special place in oriental folklore and culture. They symbolize longevity and timelessness, which is why pines and junipers are favourite subjects in Chinese paintings and other works of art, including bonsai. Most gardeners, including bonsai enthusiasts, cultivate evergreen species because they provide interest in the form of colour and structure all year round.

Evergreen and deciduous

Most conifers are evergreen. The evergreen conifers *Pinus* (pine; see pages 44–51), *Juniperus* (juniper; see pages 32–37), *Cryptomeria japonica* (Japanese cedar, see pages 30–31), *Chamaecyparis* (cypress; see pages 28–29), *Picea* (spruce; see pages 42–43) and *Cedrus* (cedar; see pages 26–27) are some of the most popular genera used for bonsai. *Larix* (larch; see pages 38–39) and *Metasequoia glyptostroboides* (dawn redwood; see pages 40–41) are also conifers, but they are deciduous.

Care of conifers

Evergreen trees are generally slower growing than deciduous species. As bonsai, they can look serene and regal. The different habits of growth of evergreen and deciduous species call for a range of training techniques, and the wiring, pruning, pinching and even watering practices used for evergreens are slightly different from those used for deciduous

trees (see pages 194–199 for more information about shaping and maintenance for the different categories of bonsai).

All bonsai conifers will in due course produce cones, which are no smaller on a bonsai than they

are on a full-size tree. It is not a good idea to allow too many cones to remain on a bonsai as this will cause stress to the tree.

In general, evergreen species are perhaps a little easier to care for than deciduous ones because they transpire (lose water through their leaves) less in hot weather, as the surface area of the leaves or needles is smaller than that of

This *Tsuga diversifolia* is grown in a natural style and planted in a contemporary container.

Above: Typical juvenile prickly foliage of *Juniperus chinensis* 'San Jose'.

Above: The twisted radial needles of *Pinus mugo*. Each species used for bonsai has its own very distinctive characteristics.

deciduous trees. Should you forget to water your pine or juniper on a hot summer's day, the chances are that it will not suffer from dehydration. The same could not be said for an acer or beech tree. For this reason, a newcomer to bonsai might be wise to choose a pine or juniper as a first tree rather than a broadleaved species.

Coniferous species

Pines and junipers are the most popular evergreens for bonsai, and each genus contains many species and cultivars that offer enthusiasts a wide range of shapes and colours to play with. In Japan, *Pinus parviflora* (Japanese white pine; see pages 46–47) and

P. thunbergii (Japanese black pine; see pages 50–51) are the two favourite species of pine. In the West, *P. sylvestris* (Scots pine; see pages 48–49) and *P. mugo* (dwarf mountain pine; see pages 44–45) are particularly popular.

When grown as bonsai, in other words when constrained within a small container, most pines develop shorter needles and internodes. As it ages, the bark of pines becomes fissured and gnarled, adding great character to the tree.

There are similarly many species of juniper that are suitable for bonsai. *Juniper chinensis* (Chinese juniper; see pages 32–33) alone has given rise to scores of cultivars

that can be used for bonsai. Some of these have adult or cord-like foliage, while in others the foliage is juvenile or prickly. There are other juniper species that are popular with bonsai growers, including *J. communis* (common juniper; see pages 34–35), *J. conferta* (shore juniper), *J. rigida* (needle juniper; see pages 36–37), and *J. squamata* (flaky juniper).

If you wish to use nursery-grown plants for making coniferous bonsai, make sure you choose specimens that have gnarled old trunks and lots of branches. You should also check that the foliage is compact, and free from pests and diseases such as scale insects and adelgids.

Cedrus

Cedar

hardy • evergreen • slow growing • easy to keep

All four species of cedar – *Cedrus atlantica* (Atlas cedar), *C. brevifolia* (Cyprus cedar), *C. deodara* (deodar) and *C. libani* (cedar of Lebanon) – make attractive bonsai. They have compact needles borne in clusters, the needles of *C. brevifolia* being particularly small. Except for plants in the *C. atlantica* 'Glauca' group, which have blue needles, cedars have green foliage. They are easy to train as bonsai in most of the recognized styles and are quite widely used by European and Japanese enthusiasts. Unfortunately, not many commercial bonsai nurseries produce or stock them.

Where to keep them

Cedars can be kept in full sun throughout the year. Most cedars are native to countries in and around the Mediterranean, although *C. deodara* is from the western Himalayas, but they grow at high altitudes, almost at the snow line. They are hardy plants in temperate climates (zone 6) and do not require protection in winter.

How to look after them

Repotting: Repot cedars in spring every two or three years into free-draining, alkaline, multi-purpose compost consisting of equal parts of loam, peat (or garden compost) and sharp sand. Cedars will not tolerate waterlogged soil.

Above: The needles of cedar bear a striking resemblance to those of larch (see page 38). Cedar, however, is coniferous, while larch is a deciduous species.

Pruning and pinching: Prune back branches in spring and autumn, cutting strongly growing branches hard back in autumn. When cutting, cut just above a cluster of needles, taking care not to cut through the needles. Pinch out the tips of new shoots with your fingers in spring and again in summer if necessary.

Wiring: Cedars can be wired at any time of the year and the wires left in place for up to 12 months, although check from time to time to make sure that the wire is not cutting into the bark.

Watering: Like most coniferous trees, cedars do not transpire as much as their deciduous counterparts and are therefore able to withstand drought much better. Nevertheless, you should water regularly from spring to early autumn and occasionally in winter during dry spells.

Feeding: Cedars will benefit from a light feed of a high-nitrogen fertilizer in early spring, and this should be followed by two or three applications of a general fertilizer later in the summer.

Be aware! Although generally trouble free, cedars are susceptible to honey fungus, which must be treated with a fungicide as soon as symptoms are noticed. Caterpillars should be picked off by hand as soon as they appear.

Cedrus atlantica

Chamaecyparis

Cypress

hardy • evergreen • quite fast growing • lush green foliage

Chamaecyparis obtusa (Hinoki cypress) and *C. pisifera* (Sawara cypress) are important timber trees in Japan, and the dwarf forms and cultivars of these make interesting bonsai subjects. The Hinoki cypress has bright green foliage, arranged in whorls along the branches, and attractive reddish-brown bark. The Sawara cypress has quite different needles (either prickly or soft and feathery), and its colours can range from gold to steel blue, although most forms have bright green foliage.

Cypress bonsai are grown mainly in the formal upright style, and good specimens can be very expensive. Examples can be imported from Japan under special licence, in the same way that *Pinus parviflora* (Japanese white pine) and juniper specimens can be.

Where to keep them

These cypresses are native to southern Japan and are normally hardy in temperate areas (zone 5), although plants may need some protection in a frost-free shed or greenhouse if winter temperatures fall below -5°C

(23°F). Cypress plants will happily survive in a full sun position throughout the growing season.

How to look after them

Repotting: These fairly vigorous trees need repotting every other year, in late spring. Use Akadama soil on its own or a mix of equal parts of loam, peat (or garden compost) and sharp sand.

Pruning and pinching: The lateral (secondary) branches should be pruned back in spring or summer. Pinch out the tips of any new shoots two or three times during the growing season.

Wiring: Wiring should be done in spring or midsummer, taking care not to trap foliage under the wire. The wires should not be left in place for longer than 10 months. Replace them if necessary.

Watering: Water cypresses regularly from spring to early autumn and occasionally in winter

Above: The fan-shaped foliage of the Hinoki cypress (*Chamaecyparis obtusa*) makes it a very attractive subject for bonsai.

during dry spells, so that the compost remains moist. Plants will appreciate being misted from time to time in summer as long as the needles are not scorched by droplets in sunlight.

Feeding: Apply a high-nitrogen fertilizer in early spring, followed by two further doses of a general fertilizer in summer.

Be aware! These cypresses are susceptible to scale insects, which can be controlled by hand if you notice them quickly enough or by applying a systemic insecticide. They also have the habit of losing a lot of their old foliage in autumn, which can be disconcerting for first-time growers. When this happens, simply remove the brown foliage by hand and the tree will look as good as new.

Chamaecyparis pisifera

Cryptomeria japonica

Japanese cedar, Sugi

hardy • evergreen • requires a lot of attention • more challenging

Cryptomeria japonica is another Japanese tree that, together with its many cultivars, is now extensively used for bonsai. It has a fairly upright, columnar habit, fibrous red-brown bark, dark green foliage which sometimes turns rusty brown in winter, and brown cones. Because it tends naturally to have a straight trunk, this species is ideal for training in the formal upright style. Untrained nursery material is not difficult to obtain, but cryptomeria bonsai are usually found only in good bonsai nurseries. Fine specimens tend to be expensive and are only rarely available.

Where to keep them

This hardy species from Japan can be kept outdoors all year round (zones 5–6). However, the foliage tends to turn brown in prolonged periods of very cold weather (although it reverts to green in spring), and to avoid this you can move your plants to a frost-free shed or greenhouse if harsh frosts are forecast. They do best in a bright, but partially shaded position in summer.

How to look after them

Repotting: Repot cryptomerias every other spring into a free-draining but moisture-retentive compost consisting of equal parts of Akadama soil (or loam) and sharp sand. Alternatively, use one part leaf mould and one part loam to one part sharp sand.

Pruning and pinching:
Cryptomerias require constant grooming to keep them looking their best. Begin to prune in late spring and continue during the growing season. Finish with a light pruning in autumn. Remove unwanted shoots from the trunk and main branches and cut back shoots that have lost too many needles and are beginning to look bare. Pinch out the tips of new shoots with your fingers constantly throughout the summer. Removing new growth from the needles can be a time-consuming task.

Above: The new foliage grown by cryptomerias needs to be pinched back constantly to prevent it from becoming coarse.

Wiring: Wire cryptomerias in spring or early summer, taking care not to trap foliage under the wire. Remove the wires when they become too tight or if you are worried about marks appearing on the branches.

Watering: These plants require a lot of water in order to grow well. In summer, you will need to water at least twice a day, and if you neglect to water properly branches may suffer from die-back. In winter, keep the compost moist but not too wet and avoid watering in frosty weather. During summer, mist plants frequently to increase the humidity around the needles.

Feeding: Apply a high-nitrogen fertilizer in early summer and a general fertilizer in early autumn.

Be aware! You will need to do a lot of pruning and grooming to keep the foliage of cryptomerias looking smart. The dense foliage can harbour scale insects and red spider mites, although constant thinning will help to keep these to a minimum. Apply a weak systemic insecticide if there are too many pests to remove by hand or get rid of them by jetting with water.

Cryptomeria japonica

outdoor coniferous bonsai

Juniperus chinensis

Chinese juniper, Shimpaku

hardy • evergreen • easy to keep • attractive foliage • eye-catching bark

Of the various types of juniper that can be used for bonsai, this species and its many cultivars are preferred by most bonsai enthusiasts. The species itself has deep green, cord-like foliage and red-brown bark; mature specimens develop gnarled and twisted trunks. Most important of all, these plants are extremely hardy and easy to keep. These trees are suitable for all bonsai styles.

Where to keep them

Chinese junipers are native to China and Mongolia, and they are hardy in all temperate areas of Europe, requiring no special protection in winter. In North America they should not be regarded as entirely hardy (zones 4–8), and in areas where temperatures fall below -10°C (14°F), plants should be moved to a frost-free shed or greenhouse in winter. Although Chinese junipers can be kept in full sun, some enthusiasts prefer to keep them under shade netting, which not only improves the colour of the foliage but also protects the plants from extremes of heat and cold.

How to look after them

Repotting: Repot Chinese junipers in early spring every second or third year, depending on the vigour of the tree. Always check the rootball first before repotting, and do not repot if the roots still have plenty of space. Never remove more than one-third of the rootball when repotting. The tree should be repotted into a free-draining compost of one part Akadama soil (or loam), one part humus (or peat), and two parts sharp sand. Or try equal parts of loam, leaf mould and sharp sand.

Pruning and pinching: There is no need to remove the main branches of an established Chinese juniper, unless you are reshaping the tree.

In that case, cut right back into the woody growth but avoid cutting through the foliage as this will make the tips brown. Maintain the overall shape of the tree from early spring to autumn by pinching out the growing tips of the new shoots with your fingers. The aim is to keep the foliage dense and tight, so avoid letting new shoots get too long.

Above: On older potbound Chinese juniper specimens, the foliage becomes adult or cord-like. There are many cultivars of this species – 'Itoi-gawa' is shown here.

Wiring: Wiring can be done between early spring and autumn, taking care not to trap foliage under the wire. Do not leave the wires in place for more than one year.

Watering: Water your bonsai regularly from spring onwards, starting with once a day in spring and early summer and increasing to twice daily in midsummer. Towards the latter part of summer and into autumn, water once a day. In winter, the soil should be kept just moist. Never let the soil become waterlogged and never let it dry out completely.

Feeding: In early spring, apply a high-nitrogen fertilizer. Continue feeding throughout summer by applying a general fertilizer every two months until autumn.

Be aware! These hardy trees need little special care, but they are susceptible to sap-sucking insects. Aphids and scale insects, which can do a lot of damage to young shoots, can usually be removed with a jet of water, but if an infestation is severe apply a systemic insecticide. Bear in mind that exposure to frost turns junipers yellow or brown. This does not look attractive, but it will not harm the tree. When spring arrives, your bonsai will become green again.

Juniperus chinensis

Common juniper

hardy • evergreen • easy to keep • gnarled trunk • black fruit

This evergreen shrub or small tree is an ideal species for bonsai. It has dark green to blue-green, prickly needles, borne in threes, and spherical fruits which ripen to black. There are several prostrate cultivars, including 'Hornibrookii' and 'Repanda', as well as many dwarf and slow-growing forms. Plants eventually develop a gnarled, twisted trunk, which makes them ideal for driftwood. They are excellent subjects for bonsai shaped in a contemporary sculptural style.

The best examples of common juniper bonsai come from wild-grown plants. Unfortunately this species is not used commercially and is not widely available. Good specimens are usually found in private collections, having been created by enthusiasts.

Where to keep them

As its common name suggests, *Juniperus communis* occurs naturally throughout much of the northern hemisphere, where it is perfectly hardy in temperate areas (zones 2–7). However, in areas where temperatures fall below -10°C (14°F), plants should be moved to a frost-free shed or greenhouse in winter. They do best if they are placed in full sun throughout the growing season.

Above: This variety of common juniper grows wild throughout Europe. It is an excellent plant for bonsai and resembles the dwarf needle juniper that grows in Japan.

How to look after them

Repotting: Repot common junipers every two or three years in mid to late spring, but only if the tree is potbound. Never remove more than one-third of the rootball.

This species should be repotted in a free-draining, slightly alkaline compost consisting of one part Akadama soil (or loam), one part peat (or garden compost) and two parts sharp sand.

Pruning and pinching: Prune back branches and old shoots in late spring, cutting back into the woody growth. Cut just above a cluster of needles, taking care not to cut through the needles themselves. Maintain the shape from early spring to autumn by pinching out the growing tips of new shoots with your fingers. The aim is to keep the foliage dense, so don't let new shoots get too long.

Wiring: Wiring can be done between early spring and autumn. Be careful not to trap needles under the wire and do not leave the wires in place for more than one year.

Watering: Water common junipers regularly but sparingly, giving more water in summer than in spring or autumn. In winter, keep the compost just moist. These plants will not thrive in waterlogged soil.

Feeding: Start feeding in early spring with a high-nitrogen fertilizer. In summer, apply a general fertilizer every couple of months. Do not feed common junipers in autumn or winter.

Be aware! These trees need little special care. Sap-sucking insects can usually be dislodged by a jet of water or by hand. If they are persistent, apply a systemic insecticide. Bear in mind that exposure to frost turns junipers yellow or brown. This does not look attractive, but it will not harm the tree. When spring arrives, your bonsai will become green again.

Juniperus communis

Juniperus rigida

Needle juniper, temple juniper, Tosho

hardy • evergreen • fast growing • gnarled trunk • purplish berries

The sharp, bright green needles, which make this species difficult to handle, are borne in groups of three on this spreading tree. *Juniperus rigida* produces purplish berries, and has peeling brown bark and a gnarled trunk which makes it a suitable species for driftwood. Variants have different needle lengths. It is an easy-to-grow species, but requires a lot of pruning and pinching if it is to look its best. The tree is a great favourite with bonsai enthusiasts, and examples are fairly easy to obtain from bonsai nurseries in countries that permit the importation of the species.

Where to keep them

Needle junipers are native to northern China, Korea and Japan. They are fully hardy in temperate areas (zone 6). Where winter temperatures fall below -10°C (14°F), trees should be moved to a frost-free shed or greenhouse. These trees grow best in full sun during the growing season.

Above: Most junipers bear fruit on all plants, but the needle juniper is dioecious (the male and female plants are distinct) and only female plants will produce berries.

How to look after them

Repotting: Repot needle junipers every second or third year during mid to late spring. Never remove more than one-third of the rootball. This species should be repotted in a free-draining, gritty compost, such as a mix of equal parts Akadama soil (or loam) and coarse grit. Some Japanese nurseries plant their needle junipers in pure grit.

Pruning and pinching: Old wood should be pruned back in early spring. Cut just above a cluster of needles, taking care not to cut through the needles themselves. When the new shoots start into growth in late spring, regular pruning, as well as pinching out of the growing tips with your fingers, will be required. Remove shoots emerging from the trunk and don't allow any shoots to get too long.

Wiring: Plants can be wired any time from autumn to early spring, taking care not to trap needles under the wire. The wires can be left on until the desired shape has been achieved, but check that they are not biting into the bark. Wires on thicker branches may need to be left in place for two or more years for the shape to set. Wrap the branch in raffia if it is very thick and in danger of snapping.

Watering: Water regularly throughout the growing season, increasing the amount given in summer. Allow the surface of the soil to dry slightly between waterings. Although the compost must never be allowed to dry out completely, it is important that the soil never becomes waterlogged in winter or the roots will rot. This applies to both indoor and outdoor trees.

Feeding: Apply a high-nitrogen fertilizer in early spring. Change to a general fertilizer in summer and apply once a month until late summer. Do not feed needle junipers in autumn and winter.

Be aware! Scale insects and red spider mites can be a problem. Jetting plants with water usually removes the pests, but serious

Juniperus rigida

infestations should be treated with a systemic insecticide. Bear in mind that exposure to frost turns junipers yellow or brown.

This does not look attractive, but it will not harm the tree. When spring arrives, your bonsai will become green once again.

outdoor coniferous bonsai

outdoor coniferous bonsai

Larix

Larch, Kara matsu

hardy • deciduous • easy to keep and train • colourful foliage

When larches are in leaf they resemble pines, despite being deciduous. In spring they have attractive pale green foliage, which turns golden-yellow in autumn before it falls. The species used most often for bonsai are *Larix kaempferi* (Japanese larch), *L. decidua* (European larch) and *L. laricina* (American larch). In Europe, larches collected from the wild are popular and fetch high prices among enthusiasts. Larches are suitable for most bonsai styles, particularly forest and group plantings, and are available trained as bonsai from most bonsai nurseries.

Where to keep them

These hardy trees require no special protection in winter in temperate climates (zone 3). In fact, they need cold temperatures to grow successfully. In central Japan, where the summers are very warm and winters are mild and wet, larches tend to languish and their needles become coarse,

Above: Larches produce cones when they are seven or eight years old. A mature specimen makes an interesting bonsai.

which is probably why you don't see bonsai larches in Japan. The plants should be kept in full sun throughout the year.

How to look after them

Repotting: Repot young trees every two years in mid spring. Older specimens will need repotting every three or four years. Use a

free-draining compost consisting of one part leaf mould, one part loam and one part sharp sand.

Pruning and pinching: In spring, prune back any side branches that are too long, cutting just above a tuft of needles and taking care not to cut through the needles themselves. To keep the silhouette trim throughout the growing season, cut off shoots emerging from the trunk and pinch back the tips of new shoots that appear from the side branches.

Wiring: If necessary, apply wire in early summer and remove it in autumn. If you wire larches in autumn, the wires will have to stay on until the following autumn. Take care not to trap any needles under the wires.

Watering: Water your larch bonsai regularly, even in winter, so that the compost never dries out. Increase the amount of water given during summer. Make sure that the soil never becomes waterlogged. You can mist occasionally, but bear in mind that larches prefer a slightly drier atmosphere.

Feeding: Apply a general fertilizer in spring and late summer. Do not overfeed larches or the needles and branches will become coarse.

Be aware! Larch adelgids (aphid-like, sap-sucking pests) can be a problem on young shoots in early summer. They can be identified by a white, fluffy wax. Severe infestations lead to yellowing of the foliage. If they cannot be dislodged by a jet of water, apply a systemic insecticide.

Larix decidua

Metasequoia glyptostroboides

Dawn redwood

hardy • deciduous • fast growing • easy to keep • colourful foliage

This handsome tree, which was discovered in China as recently as 1941, can get to 40 m (130 ft) tall in the wild. It has orange-brown bark and bright green foliage, which turns pinkish-brown, then golden-brown, in autumn. It is a good choice for bonsai and can be trained into most styles, especially the informal and formal upright styles. The species is not used commercially for bonsai in Japan, but many North American and European nurseries have produced fine examples.

Above: The foliage of the dawn redwood is similar to that of hemlock and yew (see pages 52–54), but softer and more delicate. In autumn, the colour is quite spectacular.

Where to keep them

Native to Hubei province in central China, this is a hardy tree in temperate areas (zones 4–5), although it may need protection in areas where winter temperatures fall below -10°C (14°F). Keep plants in full sun during the growing season, but protect them from very hot sunshine.

How to look after them

Repotting: Repot this vigorous tree every year in spring. Use a free-draining but moisture-retentive compost consisting of equal parts of peat (or garden compost), sharp sand and loam. Dawn redwoods are unusual among conifers in being able to tolerate waterlogged soil for short periods.

Pruning and pinching: The new growth of the dawn redwood is very soft, so allow shoots to harden before pruning. Scissors can make the growing tips brown; to avoid this, use your fingers to pinch out the tips of new shoots as they emerge during the growing season. Be careful as young shoots can tear easily.

Wiring: New shoots should be wired only when they have hardened slightly, or there is a danger of snapping them. Don't leave the wires on for longer than one growing season.

Watering: Water regularly and generously throughout the growing season. In hot weather, you will

need to water two to three times a day. You can also stand the pot in a shallow tray of water to prevent it from drying out. In winter keep the soil moist. Never allow the rootball to dry out.

Feeding: In spring apply a high-nitrogen feed and follow this with an application of a general fertilizer in late summer.

Be aware! Dawn redwoods are largely trouble free, but can be affected by mildew in wet weather. Apply a suitable fungicide. Bear in mind that this species will need copious watering in hot weather. The leaves may also be in danger of burning in very hot sunshine.

Metasequoia glyptostroboides

Picea jezoensis

Yezo spruce, Ezo Matsu

hardy • evergreen • easy to keep • challenging to train • flaky bark

This erect species has dark green needles in dense clusters, and grey-brown, flaky bark. It has long been a favourite among Japanese bonsai enthusiasts, who use plants for both individual specimens and forest groups (if used as a single specimen, the trunk must be fairly thick to be convincing). Unfortunately, the Yezo spruce is not as popular as it once was and its importation into Europe and North America is also prohibited, so it is quite a rare tree these days. Propagate from cuttings, which root easily if taken in early spring, or look for specimens in a specialist bonsai nursery.

Many Western enthusiasts have experimented with other varieties of ornamental spruce, such as *Picea abies* (common spruce), collected from the wild. These have proved just as successful as bonsai subjects as the Yezo spruce.

Where to keep them

The Yezo spruce is a hardy tree (zones 3–4), from Manchuria, Japan and Korea, and can be kept outside all year round without any special protection. Keep plants in full sun in summer.

How to look after them

Repotting: Repot Yezo spruces in spring every three or four years, but only when the tree is potbound. If you repot too frequently the internodes will become too long. Use a free-draining mixture consisting of equal parts of leaf mould, loam and sharp sand. These spruces need soil that is on the acid side of neutral; they will not thrive in alkaline conditions.

Above: The compact growth habit of the Yezo spruce makes it very suitable for bonsai, but the twigs and branches are difficult to wire without trapping the foliage.

Pruning and pinching: Cut back the long branches of Yezo spruce in spring, leaving only a few tufts of needles. Cut immediately above a tuft of needles, taking care not to cut through the needles themselves. Throughout the growing season, pinch out the tips of new shoots with your fingers. This will keep the foliage pads compact and prevent the tree from becoming leggy.

Picea jezoensis

Wiring: Wire spruces in late autumn or early winter and leave the wire in place for a year. Take special care not to trap needles under the wire.

Watering: Water regularly throughout the year, giving more in summer. Allow the surface of the soil to dry slightly between waterings because spruces will not survive in waterlogged soil.

Feeding: Apply a high-nitrogen fertilizer in early spring. In late summer feed again, but this time with a general fertilizer.

Be aware! Aphids and red spider mites sometimes cluster on new shoots. If they cannot be removed with a jet of water, apply a systemic insecticide. Sap-sucking adelgids should also be treated with a systemic insecticide.

Pinus mugo

Dwarf mountain pine, Swiss mountain pine

hardy • evergreen • easy to keep • scaly grey bark • good driftwood

This species is a sturdy, compact tree with short branches, a gnarled trunk with scaly grey bark, and dark green needles borne in paired shoots (candles). It can be used for any bonsai style, although gnarled old specimens are best trained in the driftwood style and young plants look good as informal upright, cascade or windswept bonsai. Stock suitable for smaller bonsai can be quite easily purchased from nurseries and garden centres. However, it is the larger, older trees that grow wild in mountainous areas which attract many hobbyists, and these are usually only available through specialist dealers.

Wild bonsai specimens are often 80 or more years old, and they make spectacular specimen bonsai with thick, gnarled trunks and masses of deadwood in the form of jins and sharis (see page 197).

Where to keep them
This Central European species is fully hardy in temperate areas (zone 2). Plants do not normally require any special protection in winter, although it might be worth giving an expensive specimen some protection if temperatures fall below -5°C (23°F). Keep plants in full sun during the growing season.

How to look after them
Repotting: This species neither needs nor likes frequent repotting. Once every five to eight years is quite sufficient, and as long as the tree appears to be healthy there is no need to repot. When it is necessary, repot in mid spring and use a free-draining compost consisting of equal parts of leaf mould, loam and sharp sand. Pines are not fussy about the soil, although they tend to be short lived in chalky conditions.

Pruning and pinching: Prune away unwanted branches any time from spring to autumn. Cut just above a cluster of needles, taking care not

Above: The needles of dwarf mountain pines are easy to recognise, twisted and encased in a waxy sheath at the base of the cluster.

to cut through the needles. Sealing is not required after pruning as pines exude a resin which acts as a cut paste. Pinch out the candles (elongating shoots) as they emerge in late spring. In a cluster of three or five candles, remove one or two of the strongest ones.

Wiring: Wire branches at any time of the year, except when new shoots are growing. Take care not to trap needles under the wire. The wires can be left on for up to one or two years, depending on the vigour of the tree.

Watering: Although pines usually need less water than deciduous trees, they should still be watered regularly throughout the growing season, with more water given in summer and slightly less in winter. In winter, keep the compost moist but don't let it become totally dry. The plants will not survive if the compost dries out completely.

Feeding: Overfeeding will encourage coarse growth and thickening of the branches. Apply a general fertilizer in spring and autumn, but do not feed between mid to late summer.

Be aware! Pine adelgids (sap-sucking insects) can be a problem in mid to late spring. They cover new shoots with a fluffy white, waxy coating. Although the insects tend not to affect the vigour of healthy plants, the white coating is unsightly. Spraying in late spring is often ineffective because of the protective coating. The best treatment is to spray the overwintering nymphs with an insecticide in late winter.

Like other pines, *P. mugo* sheds its old – that is, second and third year – needles in autumn. Don't panic when this happens; the tree is not dying. Simply remove the old needles by hand and the bonsai will soon look good again.

In recent years, many old specimen mugo pines have been dug up illegally from the wild. Prior permission should always be obtained from the land owner or public authority before removing such material.

Pinus mugo

outdoor coniferous bonsai

Pinus parviflora

Japanese white pine, five needle pine, Goyo Matsu

hardy • evergreen • easy to keep • elegant shape • scaly grey bark

This species is one of the most popular evergreen conifers for bonsai and has been used for centuries in both China and in Japan. It is an elegant, upright tree with deeply fissured, greyish bark. Soft needles, borne in tufts of five, are green-blue on the outer surface and blue-white on the inner. *Pinus parviflora* is suitable for different single-tree styles of bonsai, most popularly the informal upright style. Wild-collected specimens are extremely valuable, and most of the major exhibition trees in Japan are from this source.

Elegant examples of *Pinus parviflora* are greatly sought after, and most bonsai nurseries stock bonsai from this species. Two recent cultivars, 'Zui-sho' and 'Kokonoe', have particularly small, compact needles and are often shown at bonsai exhibitions.

Where to keep them

This species comes from the mountains of central and southern Japan and is hardy in most temperate areas (zone 5). In areas where temperatures fall below -3°C (27°F), plants should be protected in an unheated shed or greenhouse in winter. They can also be grown successfully In Mediterranean areas. In the growing season they should be kept in full sun.

When this species is grown commercially in Japan for bonsai, plants are normally grafted on to rootstock of *Pinus thunbergii*, which gives a strong, vigorous tree. When they are grown on their own roots, Japanese white pines are less vigorous and usually have a slightly yellow tinge.

How to look after them

Repotting: Do not repot Japanese white pines too frequently. Small bonsai should be repotted in early spring every three or four years, and larger specimens every five or six years. Never remove more than a quarter of the old soil, and use a free-draining mix consisting of equal parts of leaf mould, loam and sharp sand. Or try equal parts of Akadama soil and sharp sand.

Above: The flowers and candles of the Japanese white pine in late spring. The flowers should be allowed to blossom, but don't encourage the cones to set.

Pruning and pinching: Prune back the longest branches in mid autumn, cutting above a cluster of needles. Take care that you do not cut through any needles or they will turn brown and die. Sealing is not required after pruning as pines exude a resin that acts as a cut paste. Pinch out the new candles (elongating shoots) with your fingers as the needles lengthen in late spring. In a cluster of three or five candles, remove one or two of the strongest ones.

Wiring: Wire Japanese white pines in spring and leave the wires in place until the branches have set, but remove them if they begin to bite into the bark. Take care not to trap any needles under the wire.

Watering: Water Japanese white pines regularly throughout the growing season, giving more water in summer. In winter keep the compost moist, but never waterlogged or the roots will rot. Allow the surface of the compost to dry slightly between waterings.

Feeding: Do not overfeed these plants or the needles will lengthen and the branches will thicken. Apply small quantities of rapeseed fertilizer in the growing season.

Be aware! Adelgids can be troublesome on new shoots if left uncontrolled. Spray with an appropriate insecticide. Japanese white pines shed their old needles in autumn, which can be alarming, but simply pick off all the old needles with your fingers. The tree will soon look pristine again.

Pinus parviflora

Pinus sylvestris

Scots pine

hardy • evergreen • easy to grow • upright growth • flaky bark

Pinus sylvestris has an upright habit with a spreading crown and flaky, red-brown or orange bark. The needles, which may be blue-green or yellow-green, are borne in pairs. This plant makes a delightful bonsai, and enthusiasts have created some beautiful specimens. Unfortunately, they are not widely available, but examples are worth seeking out, and some bonsai nurseries occasionally stock semi-trained collected material. *P. sylvestris* 'Beuvronensis' (dwarf Scots pine) is in some respects even better than the species because it has small needles.

The ordinary Scots pine tends to be a leggy plant, so is suitable for the literati style. The dwarf forms of Scots pine, such as 'Beuvronensis', are more compact and therefore better suited to other conventional styles, such as the informal upright, slanting, windswept and cascade styles.

Where to keep them

Scots pines are hardy plants (zone 3), found originally throughout Europe and into temperate Asia. They require no special winter protection and they should be kept in full sun throughout the growing season.

How to look after them

Repotting: Repot young trees every three or four years in mid spring. Larger and older specimens should be repotted every five or six years or even less frequently. Use a free-draining compost consisting of equal parts of leaf mould, loam and sharp sand.

Pruning and pinching: Prune your Scots pine between summer and late autumn, removing any unwanted shoots or branches, preferably at the nodal junctions. Take care not to cut through any of the needles themselves as they will turn brown. Sealing the cuts is not required after pruning as pines exude a resin that acts as a cut paste. Pinch out the new candles (elongating shoots) with your fingers as the needles lengthen in late spring. In a cluster of three or five candles, remove one or two of the strongest ones.

Above: These full-size needles of the Scots pine display the lovely greyish-blue colour of a healthy and vigorous tree.

Wiring: Wire these plants in autumn and winter, taking care not to trap needles under the wire. Remove the wires in late summer to early autumn, when the branches thicken.

Watering: Water regularly throughout the growing season, giving more water in summer. Keep the compost moist in winter, but never allow it to become waterlogged. The surface of the compost should be allowed to dry slightly between waterings.

Feeding: Overfeeding Scots pines will encourage the needles to grow long and the branches to thicken prematurely. Apply a moderate amount of rapeseed fertilizer in midsummer.

Be aware! Like other pines, Scots pines are susceptible to adelgids. These pests appear mainly in spring and summer; spray with an appropriate insecticide to conrol them. Scots pines shed their old needles in autumn. If you pick off all the old needles with your fingers, the tree will soon regain its healthy appearance.

Pinus sylvestris

Pinus thunbergii

Japanese black pine, Kuro Matsu

hardy • evergreen • easy to grow • upright growth • scaly black bark

Pinus thunbergii and its variety *P.t.* var. *corticosa* (Japanese black cork bark pine) have always been popular in Japan as both garden trees and bonsai. They have an upright habit, stiff dark green needles borne in pairs, and dark fissured bark that gives the trunks an imposing, characterful appearance and increases their popularity. Depending on the age of the tree, it is suitable for different bonsai styles, such as informal upright, cascade and driftwood.

Unfortunately, it is almost impossible to import specimens of the Japanese black pine from Japan. Those that are sold are illegal imports. Some European, North American and Australian bonsai nurseries have grown them from seed, although they do not achieve the same quality as Japanese examples.

Where to keep them

The species is native to northeastern China, Japan and Korea, and it is hardy in most temperate areas (zones 5–6). When winter temperatures are likely to be below -5°C (23°F) for prolonged periods, move trees to the shelter of a frost-free shed or greenhouse. During the growing season, this bonsai should be kept in full sun.

How to look after them

Repotting: Repot young trees in late spring every three or four years; larger specimens need repotting every five or six years.

Use a free-draining compost consisting of equal parts of leaf mould, loam and sharp sand. Or try two parts Akadama soil and one part grit (or sharp sand).

Pruning and pinching: Prune specimens of Japanese black pine between summer and late autumn, removing any unwanted shoots or branches, preferably at the nodal

junctions. Take care not to cut through any needles as they will turn brown. Sealing is not required after pruning as pines exude a resin that acts as a cut paste. Pinch out the new candles (elongating shoots) with your fingers as the needles lengthen in late spring. In a cluster of three or five candles, remove one or two of the strongest ones.

Above: The Japanese black pine has stiff upright needles and crusty black bark that gives it a very rugged appearance.

Wiring: Wire in autumn or winter, removing the wire before the branches thicken in late summer the following year. Take care not to trap needles under the wire.

Watering: Water regularly throughout the growing season, giving more water during summer. Keep the compost moist in winter but never allow it to become waterlogged, as this will lead to root rot. The surface of the compost should be allowed to dry slightly between waterings.

Feeding: Too much fertilizer will lead to coarse growth, with long needles and thick branches. Apply a good, general fertilizer in mid spring or early summer.

Be aware! Adelgids can be a problem in spring. The best treatment is to spray the overwintering nymphs with an appropriate insecticide in late winter. Caterpillars should be removed by hand as soon as they are noticed.

Like other pines, these trees shed their old needles in autumn. Pick off all the old needles with your fingers and the bonsai will soon regain its healthy appearance.

Pinus thunbergii

Yew

hardy • evergreen • easy to train • deep green foliage • good driftwood

In recent years both *Taxus baccata* (common yew, English yew) and *T. cuspidata* (Japanese yew, Ichi) have become popular as bonsai. Used as garden trees for many years, they have only recently caught the imagination of bonsai enthusiasts. They are suitable for most styles, but particularly for bonsai with lots of diftwood. Exquisite jins and sharis (see page 197) can be created from the superfluous branches. They have lovely dark green foliage, and new shoots grow easily from old wood. Ready-trained plants can be found in most bonsai nurseries, and nursery material is easy to train into bonsai.

Where to keep them

Taxus baccata is native to Europe, east into Iran and North Africa; *T. cuspidata* is native in northeast China and Japan. Both species are hardy in temperate areas (zones 4–5), but in areas that experience prolonged periods of temperatures below -5°C (23°F) plants should be moved to a frost-free greenhouse or shed. Keep both species in full sun in summer.

How to look after them

Repotting: Repot young yews in spring every two or three years; older specimens should be repotted every three or four years. Use a free-draining compost of two parts Akadama soil (or loam), one part peat (or garden compost) and one part sharp sand. Yews are tolerant of most soil types, including acid and chalky soils.

Pruning and pinching: Prune yews in spring or autumn, cutting the laterals (secondary shoots) back

above a tuft of needles and taking care not to cut through the needles themselves. The growing tips of young shoots should be pinched out with your fingers as they emerge between spring and autumn.

Wiring: Wire from early autumn to early spring, but avoid wiring soft branches. Don't trap needles under the wire. Leave wires on until the branch sets – from one to five years, depending on the thickness and age of the branch.

Above: Yews produce lovely red berries, with poisonous seeds. The foliage of the Japanese yew (shown here) grows radially, unlike the flat leaves of the English yew.

Watering: Water regularly throughout the growing season, giving more water in summer. Although the soil should never be allowed to dry out completely in winter, do not allow it to become too wet, because the combination of waterlogged soil and frost can damage the roots.

Feeding: Apply a general fertilizer in summer. If the leaves look yellow give a high-nitrogen feed. Do not feed yews in mid to late summer, but give them a general feed in autumn.

Be aware! Scale insects can be a problem on old leaves, while young leaves are sometimes attacked by aphids. Try removing the aphids by jetting them with water. Otherwise apply a systemic insecticide. Keep yews in free-draining soil so that the roots will not be damaged in freezing weather. Winter frosts sometimes turn the foliage reddish-brown, but it will revert to green in spring.

Taxus cuspidata

Tsuga

Hemlock

hardy • evergreen • easy to keep • delicate foliage • dark scaly bark

These handsome, hardy conifers make good bonsai and suitable species include *Tsuga canadensis*, *T. diversifolia*, *T. heterophylla* and *T. sieboldii*. Hemlocks have an upright, conical habit and dark green leaves, which are similar to those of *Taxus* (yew) but more refined. The purplish-brown, fissured bark flakes attractively. They are sometimes seen in Japanese bonsai nurseries, but are not produced in commercial quantities. The most commonly available species in the West is *T. canadensis*. It is a popular species with amateur enthusiasts and can be used for most styles.

Where to keep them

Originating in western North America, this is a hardy species (zones 2–4) which needs no special protection in winter unless prolonged periods of freezing weather are forecast, in which case plants should be moved to a frost-free shed or greenhouse. In

Above: Hemlocks bear a striking resemblance to yews. Pictured here are the needles of the Western hemlock (*Tsuga heterophylla*).

summer, plants can be kept in full sun, although they will appreciate some shade from direct sunshine at the height of summer.

How to look after them

Repotting: Repot hemlocks in spring every three to five years. Use a moisture-retentive, free-draining compost consisting of equal parts of peat (or garden compost), loam and sharp sand. They prefer soil that is on the acid side of neutral.

Pruning and pinching: Prune hemlocks in spring or autumn, cutting back branches above a tuft of needles and taking care not to cut through any needles. The growing tips of young shoots should be pinched out with your fingers as they emerge between spring and autumn.

Wiring: Wiring should be done between early autumn and early spring, but avoid wiring soft, unlignified branches. The twigs tend to be very slender, so wiring should be delicate and precise. Use copper wire for exhibition trees and take care to avoid trapping foliage under the wire. The wire can be left on for two or three years, until it starts to bite into the bark. Wiring can be kept to a minimum with small-needled varieties if the new shoots are trimmed regularly and pruned hard back to old wood – in fact some hobbyists do not wire at all.

Watering: Water regularly throughout the growing season, giving more water in summer. If a tree has not been repotted for several years, make sure the rootball is thoroughly soaked when you water. Keep the compost moist in winter.

Feeding: Apply a high-nitrogen fertilizer in spring. Afterwards, change to a low-nitrogen feed and apply once a month until late summer. Do not feed these plants during winter.

Be aware! Scale insects can sometimes be a problem on hemlock specimens, but can be easily treated with a systemic insecticide. These plants are otherwise trouble free.

Tsuga diversifolia

outdoor

broadleaved·

bonsai

Outdoor broadleaved bonsai

Broadleaved bonsai are usually deciduous species, which are integral to the natural landscape of the world's temperate regions and provide an endless cycle of rich imagery throughout the year. Their bright, fresh foliage emerges in spring and, as the leaves mature, changes to darker shades of green in summer. When autumn arrives, the trees take on the colourful hues that we associate with the temperate zones. Even in winter when they have shed their leaves, the fine tracery of branches and twigs against a winter sky seldom fails to touch viewers with its sublime beauty.

Care of broadleaved bonsai

Broadleaved bonsai are in general deciduous, with a handful of exceptions such as the semi-evergreen *Lonicera nitida* (hedging honeysuckle; see pages 90–91) and the evergreen *Quercus suber* (cork oak; see pages 96–97).

Deciduous bonsai go through the seasons in exactly the same way as do their fully grown counterparts in the open countryside and in our gardens. They are colourful in leaf, and when the leaves have fallen the shapes of the branches and overall structure of the trees make them exquisite works of art.

Regular pinching is key to achieving smaller-sized leaves and a fine ramification of branches. However, the most onerous part of

Right: A root-over-rock *Acer palmatum* 'Deshōjō', the two trees grown on Japanese Ibigawa rock.

Above: Maples are among the most popular bonsai subjects. They offer great variety of leaf shape and colour.

Above: Plants with small leaves, such as hedging honeysuckle (*Lonicera*), are the right scale to make ideal bonsai subjects.

in growing acers and nothing else. Some acers are grown for their spring colour, some for their leaf shape and others for their interesting bark. Most acers are hardy and can withstand fairly low winter temperatures, and they also require relatively little care apart from regular pinching and pruning in summer. Most shaping is achieved through pruning, so wiring can be kept to a minimum.

Other popular deciduous genera that are used for easy-to-keep bonsai are *Fagus* (beech; see pages 82–83), *Carpinus* (hornbeam; see pages 76–81), *Ulmus* (elm; see pages 100–101) and *Salix* (willow; see pages 98–99).

keeping all deciduous bonsai is watering throughout the growing season, especially in summer, when plants need copious amounts of water to keep their leaves turgid. (See pages 194–205 for more on training and looking after broadleaved and other bonsai.)

Broadleaved species

The most popular deciduous plants used for bonsai are small trees, such as cultivars of *Acer palmatum* (Japanese maple; see pages 64–69), which offer a fascinating range of colour and leaf shapes. But this does not mean that larger trees and those with large leaves cannot be used. Both *Aesculus hippocastanum* (horse chestnut;

see pages 70–71) and *Quercus robur* (common oak; see pages 94–95) are naturally large trees, but they make exquisite bonsai. The challenge and fascination of bonsai lies in achieving the miniaturization of such species through standard bonsai cultivation techniques. In fact, if treated sympathetically, any tree or shrub can be made into a fine bonsai.

Acer palmatum and *A. buergerianum* (trident maple; see pages 60–61) are probably the most widely grown deciduous bonsai in Japan. There are so many cultivars, offering such a wide range of foliage colour, shape and habit of growth, that many bonsai enthusiasts specialize

Above: The shining bark of a mature silver birch is one of the charms of this popular species.

Acer buergerianum

Trident maple, three-toothed maple, Kaede

hardy • deciduous • easy to train • good leaf shape • vivid autumn colour

A popular acer for bonsai, the trident maple is a fast-growing plant, which will rapidly produce a thick trunk with lots of character. The attractive leaves turn pink in autumn, and in winter the fine branch and twig structure gives the trees an elegant outline. The species, which is often grown in the root-over-rock style, is a firm favourite with all bonsai enthusiasts. Young plants are easy to train and are widely available from bonsai nurseries.

Where to keep them

Although the species, which is native to eastern China, Korea and Japan, is hardy (zone 6), like other acers it will require some protection in areas where winter temperatures fall below -3°C (27°F). These plants like full sun throughout the growing season, but they will also benefit from partial shade at times when temperatures exceed 27°C (81°F), because strong direct sunshine will scorch the leaves.

How to look after them

Repotting: The trident maple should be repotted every other year. The best time of year to do this is during early spring, when the buds are about to break. But check the rootball first: if the plant is not potbound, there is no need to repot. The leaves will become smaller if plants are kept slightly potbound. Take care not to remove more than one-third of the roots when you are repotting. Repot into Akadama soil or a standard bonsai compost.

Pruning and pinching: Any major pruning is best done in summer, when the trees are growing vigorously and cuts heal quickly. Branches can be cut back even as far as the main trunk. To keep the tree in good shape, start pinching out the growing tips of new shoots in spring when two or three leaves have formed, continuing throughout the growing season.

Above: The new growth of the Trident maple is bronze in colour. Like the foliage of most deciduous trees, the leaves of this species will change colour with the seasons.

Wiring: Wiring is best done in spring. Do not leave the wires on for more than six months and remove them as soon as they begin to bite into the bark. Wire marks on maples are unsightly, so you may need to protect the stems with raffia. Shaping with guy wires (see page 197) and by pinching and pruning helps to avoid marking.

Watering: The trident maple should never be allowed to dry out completely during the growing season. On the other hand, do not overwater. Wait until the surface of the compost is slightly dry before watering. In spring and summer you might have to water twice a day, but cut down as autumn approaches. Do not overwater in winter, but make sure that the compost remains just moist.

Feeding: This acer is a vigorous plant and should be fed throughout the growing season. Start with a high-nitrogen feed in spring and change to a monthly application of a low-nitrogen fertilizer in late summer. Do not feed in winter when the tree is not growing.

Be aware! Aphids, scale insects and mites are the main pests. If you cannot pick off all of these pests by hand, apply a systemic insecticide, following the manufacturer's instructions.

Acer buergerianum

outdoor broadleaved bonsai

Acer campestre

Field maple, hedge maple

hardy • deciduous • easy to train • good leaf shape • vivid autumn colour

This tree, which is used extensively for hedging in Europe, has the palmate leaves typical of other maples. They are dark green, turning clear yellow or orange in autumn before they fall. The tree's habit is similar to that of *Acer buergerianum*, and the species can be used for most styles of bonsai. Although field maples are widely available, commercially grown bonsai are not often found. The species is sold quite cheaply as hedging material and will thicken rapidly if planted in the ground and left to grow for a couple of years. This is certainly one of the easiest trees to train into bonsai.

Where to keep them

The species comes from Europe, North Africa and southwestern Asia, and it is completely hardy (zone 5). Keep plants in full sun during the growing season to ensure that the leaves colour well. Field maples do not require protection in winter.

How to look after them

Repotting: Repot field maples every two to three years, but only if the roots are very compacted or potbound. The best time to do this is in late winter or early spring, when the new buds are just beginning to show. Bear in mind that the leaves will become smaller if plants are kept slightly potbound. Do not remove more than one-third of the root when you are repotting. Use Akadama soil or a commercial bonsai compost.

Pruning and pinching: Prune back old growth on field maples during spring or summer. This species

Above: The leaves of the field maple will reduce dramatically in size when the tree is confined in a pot as a bonsai, especially if it is a little potbound.

makes a fast-growing bonsai, so you can cut back as hard as necessary. To keep your tree in good shape, begin to pinch out the growing tips of any new shoots in spring as soon as two or three leaves have formed, continuing throughout the growing season.

Wiring: Wiring is best done in spring. Do not leave the wires on for more than six months and remove wires as soon as they begin to bite into the bark. Wire marks on maples are unsightly, so you may need to protect the stems with raffia. Shaping with guy wires (see page 197) and by using pinching and pruning techniques helps to avoid unsightly marking.

Watering: Water these acers copiously from spring until autumn. They may need watering twice a day in summer. Keep the soil just moist in winter.

Feeding: Apply a general fertilizer about once a month from spring until late summer.

Be aware! Like all acers, the field maple is often infested with aphids, mites and scale insects. Apply a systemic insecticide if there are too many pests to pick off by hand.

Acer campestre

Acer palmatum

Japanese maple, Japanese mountain maple, Momiji

hardy • deciduous • easy to train • good leaf shape • elegant • vivid colours

Acer palmatum is one of the most popular deciduous species for bonsai. It is a flamboyant, showy tree, which is fairly easy to keep and which will give endless years of pleasure. The species is often called the mountain maple or Yama-momiji to distinguish it from the many named cultivars that are available (see pages 66–69). In early spring the new leaves emerge a pale green or bronze colour, turning slightly darker in summer and finally flame red in autumn. The delicate form of this species is suitable for most bonsai styles except windswept and driftwood.

Where to keep them

The species, which originates in China, Korea and Japan, is hardy in cool, temperate areas (zones 5–8). It does not do well in Mediterranean or tropical areas and should not be kept indoors except for a day or two. Plants will withstand winter temperatures as low as -10°C (14°F), but only for brief periods. If prolonged freezing conditions are forecast, protect them in an unheated greenhouse or shed. They can be kept in full sun throughout summer, and will produce better autumn colours than if grown in shade. However, provide protection from fierce sunlight in midsummer so that the foliage does not get scorched.

How to look after them

Repotting: Repot every two or three years, but only if the roots are very compacted or potbound. The best time to do this is in late winter or

Above: This Japanese mountain maple is grown in the root-over-rock style. The foliage is about to reach the spectacular peak of its autumn display.

early spring, when the new buds are just beginning to show. The leaves will become smaller if plants are kept slightly potbound. Do not prune away more than one-third of the roots during

repotting. Repot into Akadama soil or a special bonsai compost.

Pruning and pinching: Prune back unwanted branches on Japanese maples in early summer, after the first flush of growth, and again in midsummer, after the second flush of growth. Pinch out the growing tips of new shoots when two or three leaves have formed, continuing throughout the growing season.

Wiring: Wiring is best done in spring. Do not leave the wires on for more than six months and remove them as soon as they begin to bite into the bark. You may need to protect the stems with raffia because wire marks on maples are unsightly. Shaping with guy wires (see page 197) or by pinching and pruning alone helps to avoid marking.

Watering: Water Japanese maples once a day in early spring and autumn, and twice or more each day in summer. Never let plants dry out completely in summer, but wait until the top of the compost dries slightly before each watering. When you do water these plants, apply enough water for it to come through the drainage holes in the base of the pot. Keep the compost just moist in winter.

Feeding: Start feeding Japanese maples once the new leaves have hardened, which is usually a month or so after they emerge in spring. Apply a high-nitrogen feed

once a month until early summer. Do not feed for a month, then resume regular feeding in late summer or early autumn with a low-nitrogen fertilizer. Do not apply feed in winter when the plant is not growing.

Be aware! These acers are often attacked by aphids and scale insects. Apply a systemic insecticide if there are too many pests to remove by hand.

Acer palmatum

outdoor broadleaved bonsai

Acer palmatum 'Beni-chidori', 'Deshōjō', 'Seigai', 'Shisio'

Japanese maple – red-leaved cultivars

hardy • deciduous • easy to train • attractive leaf shape • vivid colours

These cultivars of *Acer palmatum* (see pages 64–65) are mostly grown for their stunning spring leaf colour. The leaves of different cultivars are all slightly different in shape and colour, ranging from soft pink to fiery red. The autumn tints, however, are not as spectacular as those of the ordinary Japanese maple. These trees are suitable for most styles except windswept and driftwood.

Above: The leaves of *Acer palmatum* 'Seigai' have long lobes and emerge a delicate pink in spring. The foliage shown here is the deeper colour of midsummer.

'Beni-chidori': Similar to 'Deshōjō', this cultivar has smaller leaves and denser branching. In early spring, the new leaves emerge soft red, fading to pink and then mid green in summer. In autumn, the foliage turns red. Small leaves and a twiggy habit make this a much sought-after bonsai.

'Deshōjō': Easily the most popular of all forms of *A. palmatum*, this is an easy-to-keep and eye-catching cultivar. The foliage is a clear bright red in spring, darkening as it matures and turning green in summer. Before they fall in autumn, the leaves turn pink. The foliage is unaffected by late spring frosts.

'Seigai': Another popular cultivar, but not for the beginner. It has the reputation of being difficult to grow in the temperate climates of Europe and North America, although there are no problems in Japan or Mediterranean countries, where winters are milder. New leaves will be scorched by frost and cold winds in spring, so protect plants in an unheated greenhouse in winter and early spring. The leaves have long, elegant lobes and in spring are a soft, luminescent pink. As the year progresses they turn reddish-brown and then deep green with mottled vein patterns.

'Shisio': Very similar to 'Deshōjō', the red spring leaves of 'Shisio' (syn. 'Chisio') retain their colour a little longer before turning green in summer. The leaves change to red again in autumn.

Where to keep them
Treat these cultivars in the same way as *A. palmatum* (see pages 64–65). They will enjoy being in full sun in spring and summer, and they can (with the exception of 'Seigai') be left outside in winter

as long as the temperature does not fall below -5°C (23°F). Placing the plants in full sun hardens the leaves and twigs; allowing the leaves to emerge in the open air produces a better, clearer red in spring. If plants are kept in a greenhouse in spring, the foliage tends to be a duller shade of red.

How to look after them

Repotting: Repot cultivars of Japanese maple every two or three years in early spring or late winter, as the buds are beginning to show, only when the rootball is very potbound. The leaves will become smaller if plants are kept slightly potbound. Do not prune away more than one-third of the roots during repotting. Use Akadama soil or a special bonsai compost.

Pruning and pinching: Prune twice a year, in early and midsummer. Pinch out the growing tips of new shoots when two or three leaves have formed, continuing through the growing season.

Wiring: Wire in spring, leaving the wires on for no more than six months and removing them when they begin to bite into the bark.

You may need to protect the stems with raffia to avoid unsightly wire marks. Guy wires (see page 197) can be used to avoid marking.

Watering: Give plenty of water throughout the growing season and never let the soil dry out around the roots. In spring and autumn, water once a day; water twice daily in summer. Keep the soil just moist in winter.

Feeding: Apply a high-nitrogen feed in spring, changing to a low-nitrogen feed in late summer.

Be aware! Aphids and scale insects are the most usual problems. Apply a systemic insecticide if there are too many pests to pick off by hand.

Acer palmatum
'Deshōjō'

outdoor broadleaved bonsai

Japanese maple – other cultivars

hardy • deciduous • easy to train • different colours/shapes • novelty plants

Many other hardy cultivars of *Acer palmatum* are grown as bonsai, and most of these are now available from European and North American nurseries because large numbers are exported from Japan. A selection are described below. Most are fairly easy to shape and train, and are treated in the same way as *Acer palmatum* (see pages 64–65). Special care instructions are given below where necessary.

'Aka Shigitatsu-sawa' (syn. 'Beni-shigitatsu-sawa'): This is the red form of the variegated 'Shigitatsu-sawa'. The leaves of this cultivar are particularly attractive because of their distinctive vein patterning.

'Arakawa': The most popular of the more unusual cultivars to be grown as bonsai. Its rough, corky bark gives an ancient, rugged appearance. In spring the new leaves are bronze, becoming a spectacular bright scarlet in autumn. The trunk tends to rot on older specimens.

'Asahi-zuru': This cultivar is grown mainly for its colourful spring foliage, which is a mixture of pink, cream and pale green. In summer the pink hues fade, and the leaves tend to burn in strong sunshine. This is an interesting novelty plant, but the branches are stiff and difficult to train. Although the cultivar is hardy, it tends to suffer from twig die-back. If this happens, prune back hard to healthy tissue.

'Higasayama': The spring foliage is very attractive (pale green leaves, edged with cream and pink) and the tips of the leaves curl upwards, staying that way throughout the year. Leaves lose some of the variegation in summer and turn red in autumn. As with most variegated maples, the leaves tend to burn in strong sunshine and will benefit from some light shade.

'Kashima-yatsabusa': A popular dwarf acer with small leaves, a twiggy branch structure and an upright habit (pictured opposite). It will benefit from leaf pruning (partial or total defoliation, see page 195) in early summer to allow light into the branch structure. The branches should be thinned regularly to prevent die-back.

'Kiyohime': This dwarf cultivar is extensively used and almost invariably grown in the broom style. It has small leaves and a dense, twiggy branch structure. The branches must be thinned

Above: The fine, small leaves of *Acer palmatum* 'Kiyohime'.

regularly to prevent the twigs from dying back. This is one of the earliest maples to come into leaf, so repotting should be done early (about a couple of weeks before the other types of *A. palmatum*). Leaf pruning should be done on strong, healthy trees in early summer. 'Kiyohime' fares better in deeper containers than those in which it is usually sold. Protect this cultivar in hard winters to prevent die-back.

'Koto-no-ito': The name of this cultivar means 'harp string', and its leaves are like fine threads or the string of the Japanese harp. In early spring the leaves are a pale green, turning bright red in autumn. This cultivar is increasingly seen as bonsai.

'Kurui-jishi': This cultivar is grown primarily for the novelty value of its curled, misshapen leaves.

'Mikawa-yatsabusa': This is another of the dwarf (or *yatsabusa*) forms that are popular as bonsai. The leaves, which are mid green for most of the year, turn red in autumn and grow in tight, congested bunches. It is a difficult acer to train because the branches have short internodes and are heavily clothed with leaves.

A. palmatum var. dissectum 'Seiryu': This cultivar has delicate foliage that is a pretty bronze in spring, pale green in summer and red in the autumn.

'Shigitatsu-sawa': This cultivar is increasingly popular for its attractive foliage, variegated with clearly visible veins. The leaves turn red in autumn.

'Shishigashira': This maple has tight foliage, which is particularly attractive, and the small leaves make it very suitable for bonsai. It is usually propagated by layering (see page 203), and the cultivar can be used for both small and large bonsai. Shaping is normally done by pruning alone. It is a hardy tree which takes on a good autumn colour.

'Ukon': A fairly recent introduction used increasingly for bonsai. The pale lime-green foliage retains its colour until autumn, when it turns to pure gold.

outdoor broadleaved bonsai

Acer palmatum 'Kashima-yatsabusa'

Aesculus hippocastanum

Horse chestnut, buckeye

hardy • deciduous • easy to train • white or red flowers • novelty plant

The common horse chestnut is not often used for bonsai, but when trained well it forms an eye-catching plant that is particularly suitable for the formal upright, informal upright and natural tree styles. It has mid green leaves consisting of five to seven leaflets. White flowers are borne in upright clusters in late spring to early summer. Not sold commercially as a bonsai, the species is, however, popular with enthusiasts of novelty trees. There are several cultivars, including some with double flowers and some with red flowers.

Where to keep them

The species is native to southeastern Europe, and although it is generally hardy (zones 5–6), it should be moved to a frost-free greenhouse or shed if long periods of very low temperatures are forecast. In summer, position the species out of direct sun, which will scorch the foliage.

How to look after them

Repotting: Horse chestnuts do not need to be repotted too frequently, because this encourages the leaves to get large. Once every three to five years is sufficient. Repotting is best done in early spring. Do not overpot – that is, do not use too large a pot – because this will also encourage large leaves. These trees prefer a free-draining compost mixture which is rich in loam.

Pruning and pinching: Prune the tips of the shoots (the sticky buds) before the leaves emerge to encourage a good overall branch structure. To keep the silhouette neat, pinch out the growing tips of new shoots when two or three leaves have formed, continuing throughout the growing season. Leaf size can be reduced through leaf pruning (total or partial defoliation, see page 195) in early summer. This will induce a new crop of smaller leaves.

Wiring: This species is shaped mainly by pruning. If you wish to wire, do so in midsummer, when

Above: This is the full-size leaf of the horse chestnut when trained as a bonsai. The spotting on the leaf is typical of this species.

the twigs have just hardened.
Leave the wires on for a maximum
of one growing season.

Watering: Horse chestnuts
lose a lot of water, particularly
in the growing season, through
transpiration. You will need to
water twice a day in hot,
sunny weather. Keep the
soil just moist in winter.

Feeding: Take care to apply weak
solutions of a general liquid feed,
because too strong a fertilizer will
burn the leaves of this species.

Be aware! Horse chestnuts
tend to shed their leaves early –
sometimes in late summer –
although leaf pruning carried out
in early summer can help to
prolong the season. Nevertheless,
by late summer a bosai will often
begin to look tired.

Scale insects can be a problem;
apply a systemic insecticide if
necessary. Horse chestnuts are also
susceptible to canker, coral spot
and leaf blotch. Pick off and
destroy infected leaves or wood,
and apply a fungicide. A winter
wash of lime sulphur may help.

Aesculus hippocastanum

outdoor broadleaved bonsai

outdoor broadleaved bonsai

Alnus
Alder

hardy • decidous • easy to train • trouble free • yellow-brown catkins

Two species of alder, *Alnus cordata* (Italian alder) and *A. glutinosa* (common alder, black alder), are grown as bonsai. *A. cordata* has glossy, dark green, heart-shaped leaves, while *A. glutinosa* has dark green, ovate leaves. Both species produce yellowish-brown catkins in late winter or early spring. They make attractive bonsai, although the leaves can appear out of proportion to the tree. They are easy to train but are rarely seen in commercial bonsai nurseries, being preferred by amateur enthusiasts.

Where to keep them

A. cordata is native to southern Italy, and *A. glutinosa* is found throughout Europe and into North Africa and western Asia. Both are hardy species (zone 5), although they should be moved to a frost-free greenhouse or shed if prolonged freezing weather is forecast. In summer they can be kept in full sun.

How to look after them

Repotting: Both these alders are vigorous plants and will need to be repotted annually in early spring, but they are not fussy about the compost that is used. When you are repotting, you can remove up to half the rootball.

Pruning and pinching: During spring, prune back to old wood to maintain the plant's structure. Alders grow very rapidly, so both species will need regular pruning during summer if they are to stay in good shape. You should pinch out the tips of new shoots weekly

Above: The dark green, ovate leaves of the fast-growing common alder. These are distinct from the heart-shaped foliage of the Italian alder.

during the growing season to keep the tree compact and promote short internodes.

Wiring: Wire the previous year's growth, which will have had time to harden, because the new growth is usually too tender. The wires should be removed as soon as the branches have set in position, which may be just

a couple of months. Alder marks easily from wiring, but this is not necessarily detrimental as a rough, scarred surface lends character to the bonsai.

Watering: Water both these species of alder freely throughout the growing season. *A. glutinosa*, which is often found near water in the wild, will tolerate wet compost

Alnus glutinosa

for short periods of time. In winter, keep the compost for both species only just moist to avoid rot.

Feeding: Apply a general fertilizer to both species once a month from early spring to late summer.

Be aware! Alders are occasionally infested with aphids and scale insect; apply a systemic insecticide. Although they like moisture-retentive soil, if they stand in waterlogged soil for too long they will suffer from root rot, a fatal disease. Branches sometimes suffer from die-back; when this happens prune back hard to healthy tissue.

outdoor broadleaved bonsai

Betula

Birch

hardy • deciduous • more challenging • delicate branches • white bark

The Chinese and Japanese have never used birches for their bonsai, but two species, *Betula pendula* (silver birch) and *B. utilis* (Himalayan birch), are increasingly trained by enthusiasts in the West for forest plantings and individual specimen bonsai. It takes a long while before the bark turns white, but it will eventually do so. Birches are not usually sold as commercial bonsai, but they are available from amateur enthusiasts and through societies.

Above: The bark on silver birch only turns its distinctive shade of white when the trees are at least 10 years old.

Where to keep them

Betula pendula is found growing throughout Europe and Russia, while *B. utilis* is native to China and the Himalayas, so those are hardy trees (zones 2–3) which need no winter protection. In summer, they can be placed in full sun or partial shade. Unfortunately, birches are not long-lived as bonsai because the trunks rot easily; try replanting them in open ground from time to time to rejuvenate tired trees.

How to look after them

Repotting: Repot birches once every three or four years. This is best done in early spring. You should use a multi-purpose compost consisting of equal parts of loam, peat (or garden compost) and sharp sand. The compost used for repotting needs to be well drained, but moisture retentive.

Pruning and pinching: Cut birch bonsai back to old wood each year in spring to encourage new shoots to grow. Both species should be pruned regularly throughout spring and summer to encourage fine branching. Pinch out the growing tips of new shoots when two or three leaves have formed, continuing throughout the growing season.

Wiring: If necessary, the major branches can be wired to emphasize the shape, but there is rarely any need to do this. If you have to wire branches, only wire those that have hardened slightly. Wiring newly formed shoots can cause the shoot to die back, and wiring during winter (when the wires will chill the plant) may have the same effect. Don't leave wires on for more than a year as they may mark the trees.

Watering: Birches need daily watering from spring to autumn. On hot, sunny days they will require watering twice daily. In winter, the compost should be kept just moist.

Feeding: Apply a weak fertilizer once a month throughout the growing season.

Be aware! Apply a systemic fungicide if aphids are a problem. Branch die-back is common with these species; cut back hard to healthy tissue and prune to develop a new framework of branches. Birches are also susceptible to the serious disease honey fungus, which must be treated with a fungicide as soon as symptoms are noticed.

Betula pendula

Carpinus betulus

Common hornbeam

hardy • decidous • easy to train • attractive pyramidal shape • fluted bark

Carpinus betulus is often used for hedging in gardens, but it also makes an attractive feature plant, having an upright, pyramidal habit. The mid green leaves are toothed and turn yellow in autumn before they fall. Yellow and green catkins are borne in spring. This is a fast-growing tree which needs no special care, and can be trained easily into a bonsai in many styles.

Where to keep them
The species, which is native to Europe, Turkey and Ukraine, is hardy (zones 4–5) and needs no winter protection. In summer mature plants will do best in full sun, although young plants will benefit from a little shade from direct sun in midsummer.

How to look after them
Repotting: Repot once every three or four years in early spring, but only when the rootball is potbound. Repotting too frequently will result in large, coarse leaves and long internodes. This hornbeam is not fussy about compost, although a free-draining, multi-purpose mix of equal parts of loam, peat (or garden compost) and sharp sand is best.

Pruning and pinching: Heavy branches can be pruned at any time of year, although they are best pruned in summer when any cuts will heal quickly. In spring and summer, encourage fine branching by regularly pruning back shoots.

Pinch out the growing tips of new shoots as soon as two or three leaves have formed, and continue as necessary throughout the growing season.

Wiring: Wiring is rarely used to shape hornbeam, but if necessary it can be done in spring and summer. The wires can be left on for about a year on young branches and for two to three years on older, thicker branches.

Watering: Water freely twice a day in midsummer and once a day in spring and autumn. Keep the compost just moist in winter.

Above: The leaves of the common hornbeam are attractive but vulnerable to scorching in summer; protect them by keeping the plant well watered.

Feeding: Feed common hornbeams once every other month with a weak solution of a general fertilizer. Overfeeding will cause branches to thicken unduly and the leaves to become large and coarse.

Be aware! Aphids should be treated by a systemic insecticide. Caterpillars should be removed by hand. Hornbeams are also susceptible to leaf spot, a fungal disease. Pick off and destroy infected leaves and apply a fungicide. You should also avoid spraying or misting plants that are standing in direct sun.

Carpinus betulus

Carpinus laxiflora

Japanese hornbeam

hardy • deciduous • delicate shape • beautiful bark • vivid autumn colour

The Japanese hornbeam is a much more delicate tree than its European cousin *Carpinus betulus* (see pages 76–77). It has fine mid green, pointed leaves, which turn beautiful shades of orange and pink in autumn. The bark is particularly lovely – pale grey with dark vertical striations – which means that the trees are particularly attractive in winter when they are without their leaves. The graceful habit of the Japanese hornbeam makes it ideal for forest and group plantings, and they are also excellent individual specimens in the twin and multi-trunk styles.

This species does not grow as vigorously as common hornbeam, but if thick trunks are required, planting your specimens in the open ground for a couple of years should produce the desired effect.

Where to keep them

This species, which is native to Japan and Korea, is hardy in temperate areas (zones 4–5) but will benefit from being moved to a frost-free greenhouse or shed if prolonged spells of very cold weather are forecast. Place in full sun in early summer, partial shade in midsummer when the sun is hot.

How to look after them

Repotting: Japanese hornbeams are not especially vigorous trees and need to be repotted once every three or four years in early spring, but only when the rootball is potbound. Use a standard free-draining, multi-purpose mix of equal parts of loam, peat (or garden compost) and sharp sand.

Above: The leaves of the Japanese hornbeam are much finer than those of the common hornbeam. They are also more colourful in autumn.

Pruning and pinching: Heavy branches can be pruned at any time of year, although they are best pruned in summer when any cuts will heal quickly. In spring and summer, encourage a fine branch structure by regularly pruning back shoots. Pinch out the growing tips of new shoots as soon as two or three leaves have formed. Continue throughout the growing season as necessary.

Wiring: Although the shape is usually achieved by pruning, if wiring is necessary apply wire only to twigs and branches that have become firm. Those produced in the current season are too delicate for wiring. The wires can be left on for about a year on young branches and two to three years on older, thicker branches.

Watering: Never let the compost dry out, or the leaves will just shrivel. Water generously throughout the growing season, but reduce the amount with the onset of autumn. Keep the compost just moist in winter.

Feeding: Between early spring and late summer, feed these hornbeams sparingly once a month with a general fertilizer.

Be aware! Although this hornbeam is largely trouble free, fine branches tend to die back for no apparent reason. When this happens, cut them back to healthy tissue. Aphids can be treated with a systemic insecticide.

Carpinus laxiflora

outdoor broadleaved bonsai

Carpinus turczaninowii

Korean hornbeam

hardy • deciduous • easy to grow and train • elegant shape • green catkins

This is perhaps the most highly sought after of all the hornbeams. It is an elegant tree with slightly rounded, toothed, glossy dark green leaves, which turn salmon-pink in autumn. Green and yellowish-green catkins are borne in spring. Specimens with thick trunks are particularly impressive. Regular pruning will soon produce an attractive structure of twigs and branches. Good specimens tend to be expensive but are available from most bonsai nurseries. They are much appreciated by enthusiasts, as they can be carved with power tools to create striking hollow-trunk effects (see page 197).

Where to keep them

The Korean hornbeam is native to China, Japan and Korea, and it is hardy in all temperate areas (zones 3–5), although it will appreciate being moved to a frost-free greenhouse or shed during prolonged periods of extremely cold weather. This species does best if it is kept out in the open in full sun for the duration of the growing season.

Above: The leaves of the Korean hornbeam are smaller and more rounded than those of the Japanese and common hornbeam (see pages 76–79).

How to look after them

Repotting: Repot this species once every two or three years in early spring, but only when the rootball is potbound. You should use a standard free-draining, multi-purpose mix of equal parts of loam, peat (or garden compost) and sharp sand. When you are repotting, do not remove more than one-third of the rootball.

Pruning and pinching: Heavy branches can be pruned at any time of year, although they are best pruned in summer when any cuts will heal quickly. In spring and summer, encourage a fine branch structure by regularly pruning back shoots. Pinch out the growing tips of new shoots as soon as two or three leaves have formed. Continue throughout the growing season as necessary.

Wiring: Branches can be wired in early spring if necessary. The wires can be left on for about a

year on young branches and for up to two to three years on the older, thicker branches.

Watering: Keep the tree well watered during the growing season, watering once a day in spring and autumn and twice a day in midsummer if necessary. In winter keep the compost just moist.

Feeding: Apply a general fertilizer in spring and early summer, but in late summer change to a low-nitrogen fertilizer.

Be aware! This is a robust species which is not susceptible to disease and is rarely attacked by aphids or scale insects. If the plant is infested, apply a systemic insecticide.

Carpinus turczaninowii

outdoor broadleaved bonsai

Fagus
Beech

hardy • deciduous • easy to train • elegant shapes • interesting bark

Two species of beech are popular for bonsai and suitable for most styles: *Fagus sylvatica* (common beech) and *F. crenata* (Japanese white bark beech). *F. sylvatica* is widely used by enthusiasts in Europe, while *F. crenata* is more popular in Japan. *F. sylvatica* tends to have large leaves, pale green at first, deepening to dark green and turning yellow or orange-brown before they fall in spring, just before the new leaves appear. This species has greyish-brown bark. *F. crenata* is the more elegant tree, with smaller mid green leaves, which turn yellow in autumn, and stunning white bark.

Where to keep them
Beeches are native to temperate areas in the northern hemisphere. *F. crenata* is native to Japan (zones 6–7) and should be protected in a frost-free greenhouse or shed in prolonged periods of very cold weather. *F. sylvatica*, which is found throughout central Europe, is completely hardy (zone 4), although, as with all bonsai, nothing is lost by moving plants into a frost-free position if you are in any doubt. Both of these species of beech can be grown in full sun in summer as long as they never dry out, but at the height of summer they will benefit from some shade from direct sun.

How to look after them
Repotting: Beeches should be repotted every third or fourth year. The best time to repot is during early spring. Use a compost consisting of equal parts of loam and sand, although beeches are tolerant of a wide range of soil types as long as the soil never becomes waterlogged.

Pruning and pinching: If the twig structure has become very dense, prune in early spring, before the leaves emerge, so that you can see the branch structure. Beeches can be pruned at any time during the growing season. Pinch out the growing tips of new shoots as soon as two leaves have formed.

Wiring: Beeches are usually shaped by pruning, but if wiring is necessary it can be done between

Above: The leaves of the common beech shown here are rounded, while those of the Japanese white bark beech tend to be more pointed and serrated.

spring and autumn. Because the bark is such an attractive feature of these trees, protect it with raffia before applying the wire. Remove the wires at the end of summer.

Watering: Regular and plentiful watering throughout summer is essential, because beeches lose a lot of water through transpiration. If the compost dries out, the leaves will wither and turn brown. If this happens, cut off the dried leaves to encourage new shoots to form. Keep the compost just moist in winter.

Feeding: Apply a high-nitrogen fertilizer in spring, changing to a low-nitrogen feed in late summer.

Be aware! Beeches suffer from aphids and scale insects, which can be treated with a systemic insecticide. The branches are also susceptible to die-back if they do not receive adequate light. If this happens, cut back to healthy tissue.

Fagus crenata

Fraxinus

Ash

hardy • deciduous • fast growing • easy to keep • scented white flowers

This is a large genus, but the species grown as bonsai are *Fraxinus americana* (white ash), *F. excelsior* (common ash) and *F. ornus* (manna ash). These are suitable for most styles of bonsai, and make especially nice literati and forest groups. All have pinnate, mid to dark green leaves, which change colour in autumn before falling. *F. ornus* bears clusters of fragrant white flowers in late spring to early summer. Although ashes are not normally used as ornamental trees in the garden, they nevertheless make attractive bonsai and are used by amateur enthusiasts.

Unfortunately, ash specimens are rarely available from commercial bonsai outlets. However, this is an extremely vigorous tree and thick trunk specimens can be produced easily by growing them in the open ground or in large growing boxes. Where ash grows wild in suburban gardens, the seedlings are so prolific that they are considered by gardeners as weeds – but they make ideal bonsai material.

Where to keep them

Fraxinus americana, F. excelsior and F. ornus are all native to temperate areas in the northern hemisphere and so are perfectly hardy (zones 3–4), needing no special protection in winter. During summer these plants can be kept in full sun.

How to look after them

Repotting: Ashes are vigorous trees and will need repotting every year or at least every other year. The best time to repot is during early

Above: The fresh-looking bright green leaves are a particularly attractive feature of common ash (*Fraxinus excelsior*) bonsai.

spring. They prefer neutral to alkaline, moisture-retentive but well-drained compost.

Pruning and pinching: Prune ash back in spring, before the leaves emerge, so that you can assess the branch structure. These fast-growing trees are easy to train through pruning: repeated cutting of the apex will soon produce a good tapering trunk, and frequent trimming of the lateral (secondary) shoots will produce good branch

outdoor broadleaved bonsai

ramification. Constant pruning will be required to keep the trees compact. Pinch out the growing tip of new shoots as soon as two or three leaves have formed.

Wiring: If necessary, wiring can be done at any time of the year. The wires should not be left on for longer than one growing season.

Watering: Water regularly throughout the growing season, making sure that the soil never dries out, which will lead to leaf drop or die-back. In winter keep the compost just moist.

Feeding: Apply a general fertilizer once or twice a year. These are not greedy plants.

Be aware! Ashes are largely trouble free and are rarely infested with the usual insect pests.

Fraxinus excelsior

Ginkgo biloba

Maidenhair tree, Icho

hardy • deciduous • more challenging • vivid colour • flowers and fruit

Ginkgo biloba is one of the oldest species of tree to have survived from ancient times, although it is now extinct in the wild. The species is highly prized as bonsai in China and Japan because of the beautiful leaves, which turn yellow in autumn, and because these trees can live to a great age. Male and female flowers are borne on separate trees: male flowers resemble catkins, and female flowers are round and followed by plum-like fruits. Most ginkgos are trained in the flame shape, which is how they grow naturally. They are available as bonsai from specialist nurseries or as nursery material for training.

Above: The leaves of the ginkgo change from green to rich golden yellow in the autumn. No other tree has such unusual and lovely foliage.

Where to keep them

Ginkgos are native to southern China and are perfectly hardy (zone 4), requiring no special protection in winter, although late spring frosts sometimes damage new shoots. Keep them in an unheated greenhouse or shed if frost is forecast during this time. They will tolerate full sun, although young shoots may be scorched by direct sun in midsummer and will benefit from partial shade.

How to look after them

Repotting: This species will need to be repotted every three or four years, in early spring. When you repot, use a compost consisting of two parts loam, one part peat (or garden compost) and one part sharp sand.

Pruning and pinching: Prune old wood in early spring, before the new leaves emerge. Be aware that constant pruning can encourage suckers to proliferate. Pinch out the growing tips of new shoots on the trunk and main branches when two or three leaves have formed on each shoot, continuing throughout the growing season.

Wiring: Ginkgos do not usually need wiring because they are grown in the flame shape, which is the natural habit of growth of this species.

Watering: Water regularly from spring to late autumn, and in winter keep the compost just moist. The foliage will benefit from regular misting in summer.

Feeding: From spring to late summer apply a general fertilizer, changing to a low-nitrogen feed for the last autumn feeds.

Be aware! Although these trees are largely trouble free, aphids are often attracted to the new leaves. If there are too many to remove by hand, apply a systemic insecticide.

Ginkgo biloba

Ligustrum vulgare

Common privet

hardy • deciduous/semi-evergreen • easy to train • impressive trunk

Ligustrum vulgare is widely used for hedging in gardens, but single plants make attractive bonsai, and in recent years bonsai enthusiasts have demonstrated that ordinary plants such as this have the potential to become outstanding bonsai specimens. Not only is this species easy to grow, but the plant itself has many fine qualities. The trunks are impressive and lend themselves to driftwood effects (see page 197); the leaves are small and neat; and branches can be wired easily. This species is very suitable for the informal upright style.

Common pivet is not grown commercially for outdoor bonsai, although other species are grown for indoors (see pages 174–175). Nurseries may sell the raw material for making this plant into bonsai.

Where to keep them

Ligustrum vulgare, which is native to a wide area of Europe, North Africa and southwestern Asia, is completely hardy (zones 4–6) in temperate climates and therefore requires no special protection in the winter months. During summer it can be kept in full sun.

How to look after them

Repotting: Repot this species each year if the roots become potbound, but otherwise every other year will be enough. The best time to repot is early spring. Use any well-drained but moisture-retentive compost.

Pruning and pinching: *Ligustrum vulgare* is extremely fast growing and vigorous. Hard pruning can be done at any time of year, but is best in summer when cuts heal quickly. Cut back to the main trunk, if necessary. You will need to trim the shoots regularly to maintain the overall shape of the plant, and constant pinching out of the tips of new shoots will be required during the growing season. If you want to carve thick trunks to resemble the hollow trunks found in nature, do so in spring or summer.

Above: Like most hedging plants, the common privet is a prolific grower. It produces small-scale leaves that are ideal for bonsai.

Wiring: Branches can be wired at any time of the year. Wire shoots that have been formed in the current season and do not leave the wires on the plant for longer than one season.

Watering: Water regularly from spring to late autumn, but allow the surface of the soil to dry between each watering. Keep the compost just moist in winter.

Feeding: This species is not a greedy feeder, and two applications of general fertilizer – one in spring and one in late summer – should be sufficient.

Be aware! Aphids and scale insects can be a problem. Apply a systemic insecticide if you cannot pick off all the pests by hand.

Ligustrum vulgare

outdoor broadleaved bonsai

Lonicera nitida

Hedging honeysuckle

hardy • semi-evergreen • easy to train • neat outline • white flowers

This species is in the same genus as the well-known flowering climbers, but it is a small, neat shrub, widely used for hedging in gardens but with many characteristics that make it a suitable bonsai. The small, glossy leaves are dark green above and lighter beneath. Small white flowers appear in spring and are followed by purple-blue berries. Old plants can develop thick trunks, which make them ideal for small and medium-sized specimen bonsai. They are also suitable for carving driftwood effects (see page 197) and can be trained into most bonsai styles.

Although the hedging honeysuckle is not used for commercial bonsai, it is popular with amateur enthusiasts and can be trained without difficulty. As it is fast growing, the species can be easily propagated from cuttings, and young plants are ideal for the miniature bonsai known as *mame*. Older specimens with thick trunks are usually sourced from hedges and gardens where they have been growing for a long time.

Where to keep them

The species is native to southwestern China, and although it is generally hardy (zones 5–7), it should be moved to a frost-free greenhouse or shed if prolonged periods of freezing weather are forecast. During the growing season it can be kept in full sun.

How to look after them

Repotting: You will need to repot this plant every other year. The best time to do this is during early

Above: Even the full-size leaves of the hedging honeysuckle are small and dainty. The top surfaces of the leaves are dark green, while the undersides are paler.

spring. Use free-draining but moisture-retentive compost, consisting of equal parts loam, peat (or garden compost) and sharp sand.

Pruning and pinching: Hard pruning can be done at any time of year, but is best done in summer when cuts heal quickly. Cut back to the main trunk if necessary. Like all hedging plants, *Lonicera nitida* grows very rapidly and regular pruning is essential to maintain the bonsai's shape. The tips of new shoots will need to be constantly pinched out during the growing season.

Wiring: If you wish to develop a new branch, simply allow one new bud to grow unchecked until the branch is sufficiently thick. This can be achieved in one growing season and when thick enough the branch can be wired. However, there is no real need to wire this species as all the training can be achieved through pruning.

Watering: Water hedging honeysuckle regularly throughout the growing season and never let the soil dry out. The leaves will drop if the rootball gets too dry. In winter keep the compost just moist.

Feeding: These are not greedy plants but will benefit from applications of a general fertilizer in spring, summer and winter.

Be aware! Aphids are the only potential problem likely to trouble these reliable plants. Apply a systemic insecticide if you cannot pick off all of the pests by hand.

Lonicera nitida

outdoor broadleaved bonsai

Nothofagus antarctica

Antarctic beech

hardy • deciduous • easy to train • small leaves • vivid autumn colour

This small tree or shrub makes a most attractive bonsai subject and is suitable for most styles of bonsai. The small rounded leaves, which are glossy and dark green, turn a beautiful shade of orange before they fall in autumn. Plants are easy to grow and train. They are not often seen in commercial bonsai nurseries, although they are popular with amateur enthusiasts.

Where to keep them

This species is native to southern Chile and Argentina, as its common name suggests, and it is generally hardy (zones 6–7), although plants should be moved to a frost-free greenhouse or shed if long periods of very cold weather are forecast. Young plants should be sheltered from cold, drying winds. In summer the species can be kept in full sun.

How to look after them

Repotting: Antarctic beech will need to be repotted every two or three years. The best time to do this is during early spring. The plants require a moisture-retentive but free-draining soil, which must be lime free (ericaceous) or the leaves will become chlorotic, turn yellow and die.

Pruning and pinching: Plants can be pruned at any time of year. As this species has small leaves, you can prune new shoots in whatever way necessary to achieve the outline you want. It is not necessary to prune back to two or three buds as with species with larger leaves, such as beech or alder. Pinch out the growing tips of new shoots throughout the growing season.

Above: The attractive leaves of *Nothofagus antarctica* – or Antarctic beech – are reminiscent of the foliage of birch, rather than that of beech.

Wiring: Antarctic beech can be wired at any time of the year, but shoots should only be wired when they have hardened sufficiently. Wires should not be left on the branches for longer than one growing season.

Watering: This species will need to be watered regularly throughout the growing season. You may need to water twice a day in summer to prevent the compost from drying out. In winter, the compost should be kept just moist.

Feeding: Apply a general fertilizer in spring and change to a low-nitrogen fertilizer in late summer.

Be aware! These plants are rarely troubled by pests and diseases, although root rot, which is fatal, occasionally strikes. Avoid allowing the roots to become waterlogged.

Nothofagus antarctica

Quercus robur

Common oak, English oak

hardy • deciduous • challenging to train • attractive bark • acorns

This species, one of the best-known members of a large genus, develops into a broadly spreading tree, with brownish-grey bark. The familiar lobed leaves are dark green, and acorns ripen in autumn. When plants are grown as bonsai they look best with reasonably sized trunks, which take time to develop. They are particularly well suited to the informal upright style and the broom style. The species, which is popular with amateur growers, is not often sold as bonsai in commercial nurseries, although small starter plants can be found and some nurseries have old collected material as partly trained bonsai.

Where to keep them

The tree is found growing throughout Europe and is hardy (zone 6), although plants should be moved to a frost-free greenhouse or shed in areas that experience long periods of very cold winter weather. They can be kept in full sun in summer.

Above: The leaves of the common oak look fresh and green in the spring, but by midsummer they can have a tired appearance.

How to look after them

Repotting: Repot this type of oak every two or three years, during early spring. Use a good-quality, moisture-retentive compost consisting of equal parts of loam, peat (or garden compost) and sharp sand.

Pruning and pinching: Any pruning to shape the tree should be done in early spring, before growth commences. Prune out new shoots if necessary in autumn, before the wood has hardened. Pinching out is not essential, as oaks are not vigorous growers, and the growing bud at the tip of the shoot should only be pinched when growth has ceased in midsummer. Leaf pruning (total or partial defoliation, see page 195) can be done in early summer to induce a second crop of finer leaves.

Wiring: Wire branches in spring or summer if necessary, although most shaping is achieved by pruning. Take care not to trap leaves under the wires. The wires can be left on the branches for up to one year.

Watering: Water every day from spring to autumn, increasing the amount given in summer and never allowing the compost to dry out. Keep just moist in winter. Plants enjoy regular misting in summer.

Feeding: Apply a general fertilizer in spring and late summer. These are not greedy plants.

Be aware! Oaks prefer to be kept in fairly deep pots. They are susceptible to a number of diseases, especially mildew and oak leaf gall, and branches sometimes die back for no apparent reason. Leaf gall is unsightly but not dangerous and the best way of dealing with it is simply to remove the affected leaf. If fungal mildew affects the leaves, remove and burn them and spray the tree with a suitable fungicide. If your tree should suffer from die back, cut back the branches to healthy tissue.

Quercus robur

outdoor broadleaved bonsai

Quercus suber

Cork oak

half-hardy • evergreen • toothed leaves • corky bark • acorns

Quercus suber is grown chiefly for its thick, corky bark (which is used in the wine trade). It has toothed, dark green leaves and oval acorns. When it is grown as a bonsai, the species looks best as a large specimen, because of the size of its trunk. It is suitable for most styles, except windswept. Some beautiful examples have been created by bonsai enthusiasts in Italy and Spain with collected material, but it is not easily available as a young plant or as a bonsai outside Europe.

Where to keep them

This species comes from countries of the western Mediterranean and is not hardy (zones 7–10). In Mediterranean countries trees can be kept in full sun all year long as long as they are protected from the worst of the winter weather. In temperate areas they will need to be treated like indoor bonsai (see pages 150–151) during winter, and moved to a heated greenhouse where they should be kept under cover until late spring.

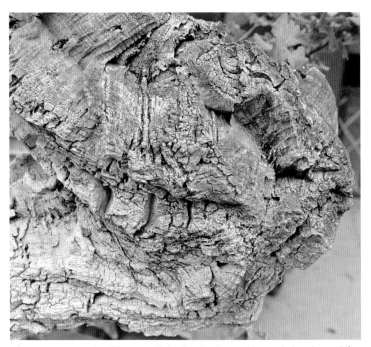

Above: A mature cork oak bonsai will develop the distinctively gnarled, corky trunk for which larger specimens are prized.

How to look after them

Repotting: Repot cork oaks every two or three years but only when the roots are potbound. The best time to repot is during spring, when the buds are about to swell. Use a good-quality, moisture-retentive but free-draining compost, consisting of equal parts of loam, peat (or garden compost) and sharp sand.

Pruning and pinching: The cork oak responds well to hard pruning, and large specimens can be made from nursery material by cutting trees back to 30–60 cm (1–2 ft). The species can be pruned at any time of year. Pinching out will also be required during the growing season to keep the tree looking trim. Pinch out the growing tips as soon as two or three leaves have appeared.

Wiring: Branches can be wired in spring or summer, but you should apply wire only to shoots from the previous year, which have hardened, to prevent scarring. The wires can be left on for a year.

Watering: Water this oak throughout the growing season, increasing the amount of water given in summer. Keep the soil just moist in winter.

Feeding: You should apply a general fertilizer in spring, and again in late summer.

Be aware! Oaks prefer to be kept in fairly deep pots. This oak may occasionally be infested with aphids and scale insects, which can be treated with a systemic insecticide if there are too many to remove by hand. Mildew can also be a problem. If the leaves are affected, remove and burn them, and spray with a suitable fungicide.

Quercus suber

Salix babylonica

Weeping willow

hardy • deciduous • easy to train • attractive shape • silver-green catkins

As anyone who has ever grown a weeping willow in the garden will know, these are vigorous, fast-growing plants with spreading root systems. The trees have slender, mid green leaves, greyish beneath, and silver-green catkins in spring. The species can be used to create attractive bonsai and is one of the few trees that can be trained into the weeping style. Unfortunately, weeping willows are not often seen in commercial bonsai nurseries.

Where to keep them

The weeping willow is native to northern China and is a hardy species (zone 5) that needs no special protection in winter. It can be kept in full sun throughout the growing season.

How to look after them

Repotting: The weeping willow is perhaps the only species that requires repotting twice a year, in early summer and midsummer. Indeed, it is so vigorous that the roots can sometimes break the pot. Use a good-quality, moisture-retentive but free-draining compost, consisting of equal parts of loam, sharp sand and leaf mould.

Pruning and pinching: The old branches need to be pruned each year in early spring, before the sap is circulating, so that the new shoots can be trained to hang down. Pinch back the growing tips of new shoots as they emerge, leaving one leaf node. Continue throughout the growing season.

Above: Weeping willow shoots can be encouraged to grow and trail gracefully by pruning back the older shoots hard in early spring.

Wiring: Wire new shoots to train them to weep as soon as they have achieved the required length. You can weight the ends of the stems to create the desired effect. Protect the stems with raffia to prevent scarring. Leave wires on throughout the growing season.

Watering: Like all willows, these plants must be kept in reliably moist, but not waterlogged, soil.

The plant's roots must be able to extract oxygen from the soil if they are to continue to develop, and this is impossible if excess water cannot drain from the soil around the rootball. Keep the soil moist throughout winter.

Feeding: Apply a weak fertilizer once a month in the growing season, except in midsummer or immediately after repotting.

Salix babylonica

Be aware! Aphids are often attracted to the new shoots of a weeping willow but can be treated with a systemic insecticide and are rarely a serious problem. Caterpillars, which can defoliate a plant overnight, are more of a pest and should be picked off by hand as soon as you notice them. If fungal mildew affects the leaves, remove and burn them and spray the tree with a suitable fungicide.

outdoor broadleaved bonsai

Ulmus parvifolia

Chinese elm

hardy • deciduous/semi-evergreen • easy to train • corky bark

Ulmus parvifolia is one of the most popular species to be used for bonsai and is an ideal plant for newcomers to the hobby. The species is variable and some forms, usually grown indoors, have smooth bark (see pages 188–189). The plants with an attractive rough, corky bark are grown outdoors. The leaves are dark green, turning yellow or reddish in late autumn, and small red flowers in late summer are followed by green fruits.

There are many cultivars of Chinese Elm to choose between, including 'Hokkaido' (which has especially small leaves and corky bark), 'Uzen', 'Catlin' and 'Nire', all of which are grown in Japan for bonsai. These trees are particularly suitable for the informal upright and broom styles.

Where to keep them

Although its common name is Chinese elm, *U. parvifolia* is found in Japan and Korea as well as China. It is a hardy tree in temperate areas (zones 4–5) and needs no special protection in winter. It can be kept in full sun throughout the growing season. Note that some plants sold as *U. parvifolia* have smooth bark and are less hardy; these should either be treated as indoor plants or moved to a frost-free greenhouse during winter and early spring, although they can be kept outdoors from mid spring to late autumn (see pages 188–189 for more on the indoor tree).

How to look after them

Repotting: Chinese elms should be repotted every two or three years. The best time to do this is in early spring. Use a multi-purpose, free-draining compost, consisting of equal parts of loam, peat (or garden compost) and sharp sand.

Pruning and pinching: Regular pruning of the twigs and branches will result in an attractive framework. If you have to remove a large branch, aim to do this in midsummer, when calluses will form more readily. The growing tips of the new shoots should be pinched out as they emerge, leaving two leaves. Continue throughout the growing season.

Wiring: Heavy branches should be wired from time to time to prevent them from curling upwards. Secondary and tertiary branches should also be wired to encourage the formation of a good framework. The wires can be left on for one growing season.

Watering: Water regularly from spring to autumn, increasing the amount in summer. Keep the compost moist at all times, rather than letting the surface dry out before watering again. In winter keep the compost just moist.

Above: The wood of Chinese elm is very dense and hard. When left to weather naturally, the bark is extremely attractive.

Feeding: Apply a high-nitrogen fertilizer in spring and then change to a general fertilizer in midsummer. Feed your elm bonsai once a month.

Be aware! Chinese elm is susceptible to leaf gall and aphids. Leaf gall is best controlled with an insecticidal spray, but aphids that cannot be removed by hand often respond better to systemic treatments. As far as is known, elm bonsai are not susceptible to Dutch elm disease, the fatal insect-borne disease that affects garden trees.

Ulmus parvifolia

outdoor broadleaved bonsai

Zelkova serrata

Japanese grey bark elm, Keyaki

hardy • deciduous • easy to train • elegant • vivid autumn colour

These trees, which are closely related to elms, are among the most graceful amenity trees from Japan, where they are used extensively for street planting. This species naturally develops a rather spreading habit. It has narrow, serrated, dark green leaves, which turn yellow-orange in autumn, and smooth grey bark, which peels to reveal the orange tissue beneath. The natural habit is broom shaped, and bonsai are usually trained in the same style. Plants are available as bonsai from Japan, and those already trained in the broom style are expensive.

Where to keep them

This species, which is native to South Korea, Japan and Taiwan, is hardy in temperate areas (zone 5). Plants can be kept in full sun for most of the growing season, although they will do best if they are given partial shade from strong, direct sunshine at the height of summer.

Above: The autumn colours of zelkova range from yellow to bright scarlet depending on the plant's exposure to sunlight and the type of fertilizer used.

How to look after them

Repotting: Repot every three or four years, in early spring. Use a free-draining compost, consisting of equal parts of loam, peat (or garden compost) and sharp sand. Or try two parts loam to one part sharp sand. Zelkovas do best in moisture-retentive but free-draining compost.

Pruning and pinching: These bonsai benefit from leaf pruning (partial or total defoliation, see page 195) in early summer to allow more sunlight into the twig structure. You should also remove any crossing branches (growing against the general direction of the other branches) at this time. During the growing season, pinch out the growing tips of new shoots as soon as two or three leaves emerge.

Wiring: Zelkovas are shaped mainly through pruning. However, branches that require special training can be wired in spring until autumn.

Watering: Water regularly throughout the growing season, providing more water in summer than in spring and autumn. Allow the surface of the compost to dry out a little between waterings, but never allow the compost to become completely dry or the leaves will wither and die. Keep the compost just moist in winter.

Feeding: Do not overfeed your zelkova, which will result in coarse growth and spoil the fine network of branches. Apply a weak general fertilizer three or four times a year.

Be aware! Sometimes branches of this species die back in winter. Remove the dead twigs in early spring, cutting back to healthy tissue. Zelkovas are susceptible to infestations of scale insects, which are best treated by applying a systemic insecticide.

Zelkova serrata

outdoor
flowering
bonsai

Outdoor flowering bonsai

Most people are amazed to see flowering bonsai. They find it intriguing that a miniature tree can produce a crop of perfect flowers, which are often followed by full-sized fruit. It seems almost unbelievable that this should be possible on a delicate little tree. Yet this is within the grasp of even the most inexperienced bonsai growers. All flowering bonsai go through the natural cycle of growth, beginning with foliage in spring, followed by flowers and, finally, fruit or berries in autumn.

Care of flowering bonsai
The plants in this group are no more difficult to grow as bonsai than they are as full-size flowering trees and shrubs. After all, a flowering bonsai is just a plant in a special pot, and container-grown plants will continue to flower whether the pot they are in is shallow or deep. Bear in mind, however, when pruning and pinching flowering bonsai that most species bear the next year's flowering buds on the current season's growth. For this reason, your flowering bonsai should usually not be pruned or pinched after midsummer, or only very lightly, unless you want to remove the following year's flowers.

Left: A pyracantha in the root-over-rock style. This species has flowers in the spring, followed by scarlet berries in autumn.

Flowering species

The flowers of some plants are gaudier than others. Most conifers and some deciduous species bear insignificant, scarcely noticeable flowers. Other plants, such as Satsuki azaleas (see pages 140–141) and wisterias (see pages 146–147), produce flamboyant, highly scented blooms.

The diversity of colour, shape and fragrance is truly amazing and is one of the reasons flowering bonsai are so popular. The main disadvantage of flowering bonsai is that the flowering period is relatively short. Most of these plants bloom for just a couple of weeks, and when the flowers are over the plants are rarely as attractive.

Plants that bear fruit and berries, such as types of *Malus* (crab apple; see page 128–129), and genera such as *Pseudocydonia* (Chinese quince; see pages 136–137), *Chaenomeles* (flowering quince; see pages 110–111), *Cotoneaster* (see pages 114–115) and *Pyracantha* (see pages 138–139) have the added bonus of a slightly longer

Above: Crab apple (*Malus*) begins to bloom in late spring.

period of interest. Others, like Satsuki azaleas, *Camellia* (see pages 108–109) and some species of *Elaeagnus* (see pages 120–121) are evergreen and look attractive whether or not they are in bloom.

A few hardy genera, such as *Potentilla* (see pages 132–133), *Crataegus* (hawthorn; see pages 116–119), *Prunus* (ornamental cherry; see pages 134–135), *Stewartia* (see pages 142–143) and *Styrax* (see pages 144–145), bear their flowers for longer, and some tropical plants, such as *Bougainvillea* (see pages 152–153), bear their showy blooms over an extended period. Nevertheless, all these plants have a limited period of glory. Like Japanese cherry blossom, the flowers are there to remind us that all life is brief and transient. The blooms are here today and gone tomorrow, but while they last we can admire them.

Above: Satsuki azaleas bloom in early summer. Their bright flowers will make a spectacular show for nearly a month.

108 Camellia

hardy • evergreen • fairly easy to grow and train • range of flower colours

Camellias are among the most beautiful flowering shrubs to have been introduced to the West from China and Japan. They bear handsome, glossy, dark green leaves but are grown for their lovely flowers, which vary in colour from white to deep red and in shape from single to formal double. The flowers are borne from winter to spring. Camellias with small leaves make excellent bonsai and are best grown in the informal, upright style.

Above: Camellias are grown as bonsai mainly for their exquisite flowers. Both the large- and small-flowered varieties are used.

Where to keep them

Camellias are found in the wild in woodlands from northern India to China and Japan, and some species occur in Java and Indonesia. Most are hardy in temperate areas (zones 6–8) – after all, the flowers appear when there is snow on the ground – although your bonsai should be moved to a frost-free place if prolonged periods with temperatures below -12°C (10°F) are forecast. If plants are outside in late winter or early spring, they should be positioned so that early morning sun does not damage frosted buds. Heavy rain will also damage delicate blooms. All camellias should be kept in partial shade throughout the growing season as excessive sun will scorch the leaves.

How to look after them

Repotting: Repot your camellias every two or three years, in early spring or immediately after flowering. Use an acidic compost consisting of two parts loam, one part peat (or garden compost) and one part sharp sand. Camellias must have lime-free (ericaceous) compost. If they are in alkaline compost the leaves will turn yellow and the plants will die.

Pruning and pinching: After deadheading to remove the spent flowers, prune back to one or two buds of the previous season's growth. If you prune during summer, you will remove the shoots that will bear flowers the following spring. Pinch out the growing tips of new shoots as they emerge, but do not pinch after midsummer.

Wiring: Use copper or aluminium wire to train branches that are up to a pencil thickness in width. The wire can be added at any time of the year except early spring, and you should use raffia under it to protect the branches. Wires can be kept on for a couple of years.

Watering: Water regularly throughout the growing season, giving extra in summer. The compost must also be kept moist in winter. Dry compost will lead to bud drop.

Feeding: Immediately after flowering, apply a high-nitrogen fertilizer. Give a second, low-nitrogen feed later in summer.

Be aware! Camellias are especially susceptible to vine weevils. Check the compost thoroughly when you are repotting and water nematodes into the compost in late spring. Aphids can also be a problem, and sooty mould sometimes develops in the honeydew they secrete. Apply a systemic insecticide and mist the leaves to clean them.

Camellia japonica

Chaenomeles japonica

Flowering quince

hardy • deciduous • easy to keep • red, pink or white flowers • fruit

This plant is a member of the Rosaceae family. It has glossy, mid green leaves and in spring clusters of red, pink or white flowers. The flowers are followed by edible, yellow or yellow-flushed red fruits. These plants are grown as bonsai mainly for their flowers. Their tendency to produce multiple stems means that they are normally grown in the clump style.

Above: The flowering quince blooms in late winter. It is a welcome sight at a time when there is very little colour around.

Where to keep them

The flowering quince is native to Japan and is perfectly hardy in temperate areas (zones 4–6), needing no special winter protection. This species will grow happily in either full sun or partial shade throughout the growing season.

How to look after them

Repotting: Repot flowering quinces every two or three years. They should be repotted in very early spring or immediately after flowering, but in the temperate countries of Europe and North America it may be better to repot them in late autumn. Use a free-draining compost of two parts loam, one part peat (or garden compost) and one part sharp sand.

Pruning and pinching: Prune back the old growth immediately after flowering and keep twigs and shoots trimmed to maintain the traditional bonsai shape. Don't prune too hard after midsummer or you will remove the next year's flowering shoots. The growing tips of new shoots can be pinched out as they emerge, but do not pinch in late summer.

Wiring: Flowering quinces do not need to be wired. The shape is achieved through pruning.

Watering: Water flowering quinces regularly throughout the growing season. Make sure that plants in small pots do not dry out in summer and keep the compost just moist in winter.

Feeding: After it has finished flowering in spring, feed this species once with a high-nitrogen fertilizer. During mid to late summer, feed plants with a low-nitrogen fertilizer.

Be aware! All plants in the Rosaceae family are susceptible to rust and fireblight. Fireblight is especially serious. Keep a close eye on the leaves for the symptoms – brown and black spots on the leaves or a whole branch turning brown for no reason – and prune and burn all affected parts. Sterilize your secateurs afterwards to avoid spreading the disease.

Chaenomeles japonica

Corylopsis spicata

Japanese witch hazel

hardy • deciduous • easy to grow and train • fragrant yellow flowers

This is one of the most delightful shrubs discovered in Japan by the plant hunter Robert Fortune in the late 19th century. Bright yellow flowers appear in early spring on bare stems, like those of *Hamamelis* (witch hazel). The dark green leaves, slightly glaucous beneath, are oval. The species is popular in Japan, but only occasionally seen in Western nurseries. It is usually trained in informal or clump styles.

Where to keep them

Corylopsis spicata is a hardy species in temperate areas (zone 6) and requires no special protection in winter, although late spring frosts sometimes damage the flowers. It will do best in partial shade during the growing season.

How to look after them

Repotting: In temperate climates in the West this species should be repotted in early spring rather than immediately after flowering, as is recommended by Japanese growers. It needs a free-draining but moisture-retentive lime-free (ericaceous) compost. Do not use alkaline compost or the leaves will turn yellow and the plant will die.

Pruning and pinching: After flowering, deadhead Japanese witch hazel to remove the spent flowers and prune the shoots to encourage new growth. The new branches will bear next year's crop of flowers, so be careful that you do not remove all of these if you prune again during the summer.

Above: It isn't just the flowers of the corylopsis that are attractive. When the petals drop, the sepals are still beautiful.

Pinch out the growing tips of new shoots as necessary, but do not pinch in late summer.

Wiring: If you wish to develop new branches, you need to apply wires as new shoots will spring upwards.

Wire as soon as shoots are hard in midsummer and leave on for no more than two growing seasons.

Watering: Water Japanese witch hazel regularly during the growing season, ensuring that the compost is never allowed to dry out. During the winter months, keep the compost just moist.

Feeding: Apply a general fertilizer immediately after flowering. Plants will also benefit from the application of a low-nitrogen fertilizer in late summer.

Be aware! Japanese witch hazel is an easy and enjoyable species to grow and is generally untroubled by pests and diseases.

Corylopsis spicata

114 Cotoneaster

hardy • evergreen/deciduous • easy to train • flowers • orange/red berries

Like many of the plants that are grown for their colourful berries, cotoneasters belong to the Rosaceae family. There are about 200 species in the genus, and many can be used for bonsai, but the two most popular are *Cotoneaster horizontalis* (herringbone cotoneaster), which is deciduous, and *C. integrifolius* (syn. *C. microphyllus*), which is evergreen. Both species have small delicate leaves, pinkish-white or white flowers and red berries, and they make attractive bonsai in the informal and cascade styles. *C. horizontalis* is particularly good for planting on rock such as tufa to make mountain scenes.

Cotoneasters are widely available in bonsai nurseries and are also popular with amateur enthusiasts for creating bonsai. They are extremely easy to propagate; young plants will grow very quickly and are ideal starter material for bonsai. Old shrubs dug from gardens are useful for larger specimen bonsai.

Where to keep them
C. horizontalis is native to western China, and *C. integrifolius* comes from the Himalayas. Both species are hardy in temperate areas (zones 4–6), needing the protection of a frost-free shed or greenhouse only when prolonged spells of cold weather are forecast. Both species can be kept in full sun throughout the growing season.

How to look after them
Repotting: Many Japanese books recommend that these species should be repotted after flowering. In Europe and North America,

however, most flowering bonsai do best when they are repotted in late winter or early spring. Cotoneasters are fairly vigorous plants and should be repotted every other

year. Repot these plants into any free-draining, fertile compost, consisting of two parts loam, one part leaf mould and one part sharp sand.

Above: Cotoneasters are grown mainly for their red or orange berries, although their flowers are also pretty and attract bees.

Pruning and pinching: Prune old growth in spring, before the plant begins to grow again. Throughout the growing season, cut back unwanted vigorous shoots as they appear. Pinch out the growing tips of new shoots as they emerge, but do not pinch after midsummer because you will remove the flowering shoots that produce the flowers for the next year.

Wiring: Wire the trunk and branches of cotoneasters in spring, before the buds emerge. Protect soft branches with raffia. The wiring should be left on the branches for no more than one year or growing season.

Watering: Cotoneasters need to be watered regularly and special care should be taken with smaller bonsai as they should never be allowed to dry out. When plants are in flower, take care not to wet the flowers, which are easily damaged. Keep the compost just moist in winter.

Feeding: Feed cotoneasters after they have flowered. In spring and early summer use a general fertilizer, changing to a low-nitrogen fertilizer in late summer.

Be aware! Like most members of the Rosaceae family, cotoneasters are susceptible to rust and fireblight. Fireblight is a potentially serious disease; if you notice that shoots are turning black and leaves are withering as if they have been burned, you need to take immediate action. Remove and burn all affected parts of the plant, and remember to disinfect your secateurs.

Cotoneaster horizontalis

outdoor flowering bonsai

Crataegus laevigata

Midland hawthorn, red hawthorn

hardy • deciduous • easy to train • pink or red flowers

Crataegus laevigata (syn. *C. oxyacantha*) is not as vigorous as *C. monogyna* (see pages 118–119), but hardy nonetheless. Different varieties and cultivars bear single or double flowers and range in colour from pink to deep red. *C. laevigata* does not set fruit as easily as *C. monogyna*. Many bonsai nurseries now stock this species, and bonsai can also easily be made from plants propagated at home.

Where to keep them

Crataegus laevigata is native to Europe and eastwards to India, and it is hardy (zone 5). Although this species can be kept in full sun throughout the growing season, It will benefit from being given some shade in very hot weather. Protect flower buds from late spring frosts.

How to look after them

Repotting: This species of hawthorn should be repotted every three or four years in early spring. Use a mixture of two parts loam, one part peat (or garden compost) and one part sharp sand. Hawthorns are not fussy about the type of soil, but it must be free draining.

Pruning and pinching: After flowering, prune back old shoots to encourage the growth of new flowering shoots. Take care to leave some of the old shoots if you want to encourage berries. Many new shoots will grow from the existing branches; these carry next year's flowering buds. Prune or pinch out the growing tips as

Above: The flowers of the red hawthorn are really charming, rather like miniature posies. Pictured here is one of the double pink forms.

necessary to maintain the shape, but avoid excessive pruning or pinching after midsummer.

Wiring: New shoots can be wired in mid to late summer. The wiring should not be left on for longer than one year.

Watering: Hawthorns should be watered regularly, especially throughout the growing season. Do not allow the compost to dry out completely at any time, because this can lead to die-back. Be sure to keep the compost just moist in winter.

Feeding: Apply a general fertilizer immediately after flowering, and follow this with a low-nitrogen feed in late summer.

Be aware! Because most examples of *C. laevigata* are grafted, you must remove any suckers that develop from the roots as soon as you notice them. *C. laevigata* is also susceptible to rust and black spot (the same diseases that affect roses). Spray with appropriate fungicides to provide effective control.

The species also tends to suffer from die-back of the crown, which may be due to insufficient water in summer or too shallow a pot. If die-back occurs, you can either use the dead branches as driftwood effects or cut it out completely and wait for new shoots to grow.

Crataegus laevigata

outdoor flowering bonsai

Crataegus monogyna

Common hedging hawthorn

hardy • deciduous • easy to train • red, pink or white flowers • red berries

The common hedging hawthorn makes a lovely bonsai. This plant is hardy, vigorous and easy to train, and it flowers and produces berries in abundance. Old plants with attractive gnarled trunks can be found in hedgerows, and they make excellent bonsai specimens. This is a favourite species with bonsai enthusiasts, and nurseries stock the plants as partly trained material and finished bonsai. The small, spiny trees are often used for hedging in gardens, and there are several cultivars. They bear attractive red, pink or white flowers and red berries.

Above: The red, pink or white flowers of the common hedging hawthorn are followed by beautiful red berries which prolong the season of interest.

It is possible to find wonderful specimens of common hedging hawthorn, with very attractive, gnarled trunks, growing in the wild. Always seek permission from the landowner or local authority before collecting wild material.

Where to keep them
Common hedging hawthorn is found throughout Europe. It is a vigorous, perfectly hardy species (zone 4) and can be kept in full sun throughout the growing season. It doesn't need any protection in winter, but flower buds should be sheltered from late spring frosts.

How to look after them
Repotting: Repot this species of hawthorn every three or four years in early spring. Use a mixture of two parts loam, one part peat (or garden compost) and one part sharp sand. Hawthorns are not fussy about the type of soil, but it must be free draining.

Pruning and pinching: After flowering, prune back some of the old shoots to encourage new growth, taking care to leave enough old shoots to produce a good crop of berries. Many new shoots will grow from the existing branches; these carry next year's flowering buds. Prune or pinch out the growing tips as necessary to maintain the shape of the tree, but avoid excessive pruning or pinching after midsummer.

Wiring: New shoots can be wired in mid to late summer. Wires should not be left on for longer than a year.

Watering: Water hawthorns regularly, especially throughout the growing season. Do not allow the compost to dry out, because this can lead to die-back, and keep the compost just moist in winter.

Feeding: Apply a general fertilizer immediately after flowering, and follow this with a low-nitrogen feed in late summer.

Be aware! This species can be susceptible to mildew in wet summers. Spray with an appropriate fungicide.

Crataegus monogyna

Elaeagnus

hardy • deciduous/evergreen • easy to keep • fragrant flowers • red fruit

Two species of elaeagnus are commonly grown as bonsai. Both have dark green leaves, silvery beneath, and bear fragrant flowers in autumn, which are followed by fruits that ripen to red and persist until the following year. *Elaeagnus multiflora* is a deciduous shrub; *E. pungens* (Gumi) is evergreen, and many cultivars have been developed from it. These plants are suitable for the informal upright style. They are popular for bonsai in Japan, where they are grown for their flowers and attractive fruit, but are less well known in the West.

Above: Elaeagnus multiflora produces scented flowers in late spring. The flowers are followed by red fruit.

Where to keep them

Both *E. pungens* and *E. multiflora*, which come from China and Japan, are completely hardy in temperate areas (zones 4–7) and need no special winter protection. In summer they can be kept in full sun, and *E. pungens* in particular will lose the silvery sheen on its leaves if it is grown in shade.

How to look after them

Repotting: Both species of elaeagnus need repotting only every three or four years. The best time to do this is during early spring. You should repot the plants in a free-draining, fertile compost consisting of two parts loam, one part leaf mould and one part sharp sand.

Pruning and pinching: The aim of pruning these shrubs is to keep the internodes short. Both species are mostly pruned in summer, after flowering, when new shoots are cut back to maintain the overall framework of the bonsai. Pinch out the growing tips of new shoots as necessary, ensuring that you don't remove all of next year's buds.

Wiring: The main branches need wiring as new shoots tend to grow upwards. Wire in midsummer when the new shoots have just hardened, and keep the wires on for one year or growing season.

Watering: Water regularly throughout the growing season, allowing the surface of the compost to dry slightly before the next watering, although you should make sure that the rootball never dries out completely. Keep *E. pungens* moist in winter, and *E. multiflora* only just moist.

Feeding: These plants will appreciate the application of a high-nitrogen feed in spring. Change to a low-nitrogen fertilizer in late summer, but do not feed in autumn or winter.

Be aware! Elaeagnus are susceptible to the fungal disease coral spot. Spray with an appropriate fungicide if you notice the symptoms. They are also often infested with scale insects, which can be treated with a systemic insecticide.

Elaeagnus pungens

Forsythia

outdoor flowering bonsai

hardy • deciduous • easy to keep • yellow flowers

Forsythias are among the most colourful of the early flowering shrubs, and they are common garden plants, the familiar yellow flowers appearing on bare stems in spring. Both *Forsythia* x *intermedia* and *F. suspensa* (golden bell) are used as bonsai in Japan and are suitable for the informal, cascade and root-over-rock styles. They are sometimes available as bonsai in bonsai nurseries. Large trunk specimens can also be made from established garden plants. Choose one with interesting roots or trunk and trim it back to the desired size. New shoots will grow from the old wood and can be wired when hard.

Where to keep them

Forsythias are hardy plants in temperate areas (zone 4) and they need no special winter protection. Keep these plants in full sun throughout the year.

How to look after them

Repotting: Repot every other year in early spring into a free-draining, fertile compost, with equal parts loam, peat (or garden compost) and sharp sand.

Above: Trim back forsythia's long new shoots in midsummer to encourage the laterals to develop as shown here. These shoots will carry the next year's flowers.

Pruning and pinching: The old shoots that carried the current season's flowers should be pruned immediately after flowering to encourage new flowering shoots to grow. Prune any long new shoots to keep the plant in shape and stimulate the production of laterals (secondary branches). Pinch out the growing tips of these when two or three leaves have formed, but avoid excessive pinching after midsummer to ensure you do not remove the next year's flowering buds.

Wiring: It is not necessary to wire forsythia if you are happy with the existing shape. If you need to wire those that are growing in the wrong direction, leave the wires on for only one year.

Watering: Forsythia should be watered regularly throughout the growing season. Make sure that the compost is not allowed to dry out completely, especially during

autumn, when the flower buds are forming for the next year. Keep the compost just moist in winter.

Feeding: Apply a general fertilizer after flowering. Plants will also benefit from a low-nitrogen feed in late summer.

Be aware! Aphids are sometimes a problem for this species, but usually in such limited numbers that they can be removed by hand. Forsythia are not long-lived as bonsai, because their trunks tend to rot with age. When the rot has gone too far, it is best to start again with a young plant.

Forsythia intermedia

Ilex serrata

Japanese holly, Japanese winterberry

half-hardy • deciduous • challenging • bright red winter berries

This deciduous holly is grown for its bright red berries. It has small, oval, pointed leaves, which turn slightly yellow in autumn. Male and female flowers are borne on separate plants, so it is important to distinguish between the sexes when buying a plant. For fruit to set, plants of both sexes are needed for effective pollination. It is a popular bonsai in Japan, and fine specimens are in the informal style with tapering trunks and a good root base. They are available from bonsai nurseries in the West only occasionally. This is not a plant for beginners.

Where to keep them

The species is native to Japan and China, but it is not hardy (zones 7–8) and will require protection in a frost-free greenhouse or shed in winter and spring. Keep plants in full sun in summer and autumn.

How to look after them

Repotting: Repot this holly every two or three years. The best time of year to do this is during early spring. Use a moisture-retentive but free-draining compost, consisting of equal parts of loam, peat (or garden compost) and sharp sand.

Pruning and pinching: Prune any long new shoots in early summer and prune again very lightly in autumn to maintain the plant's overall shape. The next year's flowers are borne on the current season's shoots, so take care not to prune off all your potential flowers. Pinch out some of the new buds as

Above: The tiny red berries of the Japanese holly are delightful. They remain on the plant after all the leaves have shed.

they form, but leave others until the leaves have hardened.

Wiring: Wire branches in midsummer. The wires should not be left on for longer than one year.

Watering: It is crucial that these plants are watered regularly throughout the growing season. If the rootball is allowed to dry out even briefly the tree will die. Keep the compost just moist in winter.

outdoor flowering bonsai

Feeding: Apply a general fertilizer after the fruits have set. Plants will benefit from a low-nitrogen fertilizer in late summer.

Be aware! Aphids sometimes attack young shoots but can usually be controlled by hand. Use a systemic insecticide if the problem persists.

As Japanese holly is grown mainly for its attractive berries, check with nursery staff that the tree you are buying is indeed a female. You will also need to source a male plant for pollination.

If you cannot obtain a male plant, then the next best thing is to place your bonsai in close proximity to an ordinary holly. There is a good chance that this will lead to a successful pollination.

Ilex serrata

Jasminum nudiflorum

Winter jasmine

hardy • deciduous • easy to keep • yellow winter flowers

This is one of the few shrubs to flower in the middle of winter. The yellow blooms appear on the bare stems in late autumn and sometimes continue right until late winter or early spring. Although the young stems are rather lax and garden-grown plants are usually trained against a trellis or along wires, the mature stems are thick and have a tree-like appearance, which makes this a suitable species for bonsai. Plants can be trained in the informal and cascade styles, and are popular in Japan as *shohin* (small) and *mame* (miniature) bonsai. They are available from commercial bonsai nurseries.

Where to keep them

The species, which comes originally from western China, is completely hardy (zones 3–4) and winter protection is unnecessary. Keep plants in full sun throughout the growing season.

How to look after them

Repotting: Winter jasmine is one of the few species that are best repotted after flowering. They are fairly slow-growing plants, and repotting every other year in early spring, after the winter flowering, will be sufficient. Use a loam-based compost composed of two parts loam, one part leaf mould (garden compost or peat) and one part sand. Fine Akadama is a good substitute for loam.

Pruning and pinching: The shoots that carried the current season's flowers should be pruned immediately after flowering to encourage new ones to grow. Prune new shoots once they have

reached the desired length, to stimulate the production of laterals (secondary branches). Pinch out the growing tips of those when three to four leaves have formed, to encourage the production of flowering buds. In late summer, take care not to remove the buds.

Wiring: If necessary, wire from spring to summer, protecting the delicate stems with raffia.

Watering: Water winter jasmine freely throughout the growing season, taking particular care that the compost does not dry out in

Above: The leaves of winter jasmine (*Jasminum nudiflorum*) are divided into three long oval leaflets. The flowers appear in the leaf axils along the bare stems.

autumn, when the flower buds will be forming for next year. Keep the compost moist in winter.

Feeding: Apply a general fertilizer in midsummer, four to six weeks after repotting. Apply a low-nitrogen fertilizer in early autumn.

Be aware! Vine weevils can be a problem. Check the compost when you repot and water nematodes into the soil in late spring. Aphids sometimes attack young shoots, but can usually be removed by hand. Use a systemic insecticide if the problem persists.

The lack of woody stems and branches makes winter jasmine harder than some other species to train as bonsai, but the long, thin shoots can be shortened to make them look more rigid and branch-like and the main stem can be allowed to thicken to give the semblance of age. However, the shape of this bonsai is less important than its winter blossom.

Jasminum nudiflorum

outdoor flowering bonsai

Malus

Crab apple, Hime ringo, Hana-kaido

hardy • deciduous • easy to keep • pretty flowers • colourful autumn fruit

Many species of *Malus* can be used for bonsai, and the most popular ones include *M. baccata* (Siberian crab apple), *M. floribunda* (Japanese crab apple), *M. halliana* (Hall's crab apple) and *M. x micromalus* (Makino or Kaido crab apple). They are grown for both their attractive flowers and delightful, small fruit, which are the right scale for the bonsai. These plants are either self-pollinating or they can pollinate other *Malus* species nearby.

Malus are suitable for most bonsai styles except windswept, driftwood, forest and literati. They are popular as bonsai in Japan, but many cannot be imported into Europe and North America.

Where to keep them
These hardy plants (zones 4–6) need no special protection in winter and can be kept in full sun throughout the growing season.

How to look after them
Repotting: Repot crab apples every other year in early spring. Use a multi-purpose, free-draining compost or one that consists of equal parts loam and sharp sand.

Pruning and pinching: Prune back crab apples in late summer, after the new shoots have formed, cutting back to two or three nodes or leaves. Pinching out the growing tips of the lateral (secondary) shoots will channel the energy of

Above: Crab apple flowers come in many colours, ranging from pale pink fading to white, to dark pink or deep red.

the plant into flower bud production and keep the bonsai looking trim. Be careful not to prune or pinch off next year's flower buds, which are usually formed in midsummer.

Wiring: If you feel it is necessary to wire your crab apple bonsai, apply the wires any time from spring to autumn. You may need to use raffia under the wires to protect the bark from damage.

Watering: Crab apples should be watered regularly throughout the growing season. Take special care during summer to ensure that the compost does not dry out. During winter, the compost should be kept just moist.

Feeding: Apply a general fertilizer after the fruits have set in midsummer. You can encourage flower buds to form by feeding the plant in late summer with a low-nitrogen fertilizer. Never fertilize immediately after flowering because this will cause the newly set fruit to drop.

Be aware! Crab apples can suffer from infestations of aphids, which can be treated with a systemic insecticide or picked off by hand. They are also susceptible to rust and canker. Spray with an appropriate fungicide. If mildew occurs, improve the ventilation by standing the tree in a more open environment and spray with an appropriate fungicide. Always burn infected leaves.

Malus baccata

Morus

Mulberry

hardy • deciduous • easy to keep and train • pink and red fruit

Morus alba (white mulberry) and *M. nigra* (black mulberry) are grown mainly for their fruits. *M. alba* is a spreading tree with glossy, bright green leaves and white fruits, which ripen to pink and red. *M. nigra* is more rounded in habit, with mid green leaves and green, rather acidic fruits. These species are especially suitable for bonsai, because the leaves and fruit reduce in size when the trees are grown in pots. They are suitable for the informal upright style with a thick trunk (the trunks on old specimens are rugged and full of character). Mulberries are available as bonsai in nurseries.

Where to keep them

M. alba is native to China, and *M. nigra* is believed to have come originally from southwestern Asia, but both species are hardy in temperate areas (zones 6–7). However, both the mulberries will need to be protected from penetrating frosts in winter because their fleshy roots can rot. To thrive, these bonsai should be kept in full sun throughout the growing season.

How to look after them

Repotting: Mulberries are slow-growing trees. They will need repotting every other year and the best time to do this is during early spring. Repot them into a free-draining but moisture-retentive compost consisting of equal parts of loam, peat (or garden compost) and sharp sand.

Pruning and pinching: Prune for shape in early spring, and again after flowering in mid to late summer, when the shoots have grown too long. Pruning and pinching back to two or three new leaves will keep the tree in shape and encourage new shoots. Take care not to remove all of the next year's flowering buds, which are formed during the previous growing season. Some of the old shoots that bore the current year's fruit should also be removed, to encourage new ones to grow. If you want to create driftwood effects by hollowing out the thick trunks (see page 197), do so during spring and summer when the tree is in vigorous growth and will recover quickly.

Above: Mulberry flowers are insignificant, but the colourful fruits are certainly attractive and even edible, though rather small in size.

Wiring: The branches of larger mulberry specimens will need to be wired. Small trees that have short branches need not be wired. Wiring should be done when the new shoots have hardened in midsummer. Leave the wire on until the end of the growing season.

Watering: Water mulberries regularly throughout the growing season, especially during summer, and keep the compost just moist throughout winter.

Feeding: Apply a general fertilizer in midsummer, changing to a low-nitrogen one in late summer.

Be aware! Caterpillars can defoliate mulberrry plants. Pick these pests off by hand as soon as you notice them. Aphids can also be removed by hand or with a jet of water, or they can be treated with a systemic insecticide if they become a problem. Fungicidal sprays may be needed to combat coral spot and canker.

Morus nigra 'Nana'

Potentilla fruticosa

Potentilla, cinquefoil

hardy • deciduous • easy to keep • range of flower colours • flaky bark

This popular garden shrub has small leaves and lovely yellow, saucer-shaped flowers. Many cultivars with different coloured flowers have been developed. Potentillas make excellent bonsai with either slender or thick trunks, and the flaking bark creates added interest. They are suitable for the informal upright, cascade and literati styles. Potentillas flower throughout the summer on the current season's shoots. They are extremely popular as bonsai in Japan, and older specimens are valuable. They are widely available from bonsai nurseries.

Where to keep them

Potentillas are found in Europe, northern Asia and North America, and they are hardy in temperate areas (zones 2–8). They require no special protection in winter and can be kept in full sun throughout the growing season.

How to look after them

Repotting: Repot this species every other year, during early spring. Use a general purpose, free-draining compost consisting of one part loam, one part peat (or garden compost) and two parts sharp sand.

Pruning and pinching: After flowering has finished in late summer, prune back long shoots. Pinching out the growing tips of the lateral (secondary) shoots when two or three new leaves emerge will stimulate new flowering shoots. New shoots on the lateral branches will bear next year's crop of flowers, so do not prune these hard back in late summer. A light trim will do.

Wiring: Potentillas don't need much wiring. If required, wire hardened shoots in late summer.

Watering: Water regularly during the growing season and keep the compost just moist in winter.

Feeding: Apply a general fertilizer once a month from spring through to late summer.

Be aware! Potentillas are relatively trouble free and have a reputation for being difficult to kill.

Above: Like buttercups, potentilla flowers always look fresh and lovely. Deadheading spent flowers will encourage a continuous crop during summer.

Potentilla fruticosa

134 Ornamental cherry

hardy to frost hardy • deciduous • pretty flowers • autumn fruits

This is a very large genus, which includes *P. armeniaca* (apricot), *P. cerasifera* (cherry plum), *P. incisa* (Fuji cherry), *P. mume* (Japanese apricot), *P. persica* (peach), *P. serrulata* (oriental cherry), *P. spinosa* (blackthorn, sloe), *P.* x *subhirtella* 'Autumnalis', *P. tomentosa* (downy cherry) and *P.* x *yedoensis* (Yoshino cherry). Most are spring-flowering trees, but *P.* x *subhirtella* flowers from late autumn to early spring, and *P. mume* flowers in late winter to early spring on bare branches with highly scented flowers. They all make excellent bonsai, but *P. mume* is the most highly prized.

All these species are suitable for most styles including windswept and literati because old specimens have gnarled and twisted trunks. Unfortunately, many countries prohibit the importation of this genus and prunus are seldom seen in the West – although you are almost certain to find one among the best exhibits at the major bonsai shows in Japan.

Where to keep them
Most of these ornamental trees are completely hardy (zones 4–6) and require no special protection in winter. However, *P. armeniaca*, *P. dulcis* (almond), *P. mume* and *P. persica* are not reliably hardy (zones 8–9) and should be kept in a frost-free greenhouse or shed in winter. All can be kept in full sun throughout the growing season.

How to look after them
Repotting: Repot every other year into a free-draining compost consisting of two parts loam and

Above: Most plants of the prunus family have attractive flowers and fruit. The sloe (*Prunus spinosa*) shown here is no exception.

one of sharp sand to which has been added a little bonemeal and a sprinkling of lime. As with most of the spring-flowering plants, repot in early spring.

Pruning and pinching: Prune immediately after flowering to encourage new growth. Lightly cut back or pinch out the growing tips of the long shoots in early autumn.

Avoid pruning or pinching out during summer, as this is when the flowering shoots for the following year are produced.

Wiring: Wire in spring to summer, taking care that you do not damage the bark or knock off the developing flower buds. The wires can be left on for one year.

Watering: Water regularly throughout the growing season, especially in summer, and keep the compost just moist in winter. Take care when watering that you do not splash water on the petals, which are easily damaged.

Feeding: Apply a general fertilizer in spring, and follow this with a low-nitrogen fertilizer in late summer. Because most plants in this genus bear stoned fruit, they benefit from a fertilizer with a high calcium content.

Be aware! Like many other members of the Rosaceae family, these plants are susceptible to rust. Spray with an appropriate fungicide if you notice the symptoms. Aphids can be removed by hand, or treated with a systemic insecticide if they become a problem. It is best to pick caterpillars off by hand.

Prunus incisa

Pseudocydonia sinensis

Chinese quince

half-hardy • deciduous • more challenging • pink flowers • unusual fruit

Formerly *Cydonia sinensis*, this member of the Rosaceae family is closely related to *Chaenomeles japonica* (Japanese quince). It has large leaves, which turn rich orange in the autumn. The flowers appear in early spring and are a delightful shade of pink, while the large fruits are oval and turn golden-yellow as they ripen. The bark flakes and peels attractively. This is not among the easiest of bonsai to keep. It is suitable only for the informal and formal upright styles. Some countries prohibit the importation of this species, so plants may not be easily available.

outdoor flowering bonsai

Where to keep them

This species, which is native to China, is not reliably hardy (zones 6–7) and will need some protection in winter. Keep your plants in an unheated greenhouse, or a heated greenhouse if the temperature is likely to fall below -5°C (23°F). It can be kept in full sun throughout the growing season.

How to look after them

Repotting: Chinese quinces should be repotted every other year. The best time of year to do this is during early spring. Use a free-draining compost consisting of two parts loam, one part peat (or garden compost) and one part sharp sand.

Pruning and pinching: New shoots will grow immediately after flowering. Leave these to extend until midsummer and then cut off the tips to stimulate the growth of lateral (secondary) shoots. In late summer, pinch out the growing tips of these, as two or three new leaves emerge. The new shoots will bear next year's crop of flowers, so do not remove all the buds. The quinces are borne on old shoots that flowered in the current season.

Above: The large edible fruits of the Chinese quince stay on the tree for a long time. At bonsai shows in Japan, they are always a talking point.

Pseudocydonia sinensis

Wiring: The best time to wire the branches is in midsummer. The wires can be left on for one year.

Watering: Water regularly and generously throughout the growing season, and never let the soil around the rootball dry out. Keep the soil just moist in winter.

Feeding: Feed these quinces only after the fruit has set. If you feed too early, the young qinces will drop off. Apply a general fertilizer in early summer and follow this with a low-nitrogen fertilizer in late summer.

Be aware! Scale insects can be a problem and are best treated with a systemic insecticide. Look out for vine weevil larvae when you are repotting. Kill any that you find and water nematodes into the compost during late spring.

outdoor flowering bonsai

Pyracantha angustifolia

Firethorn

half-hardy • evergreen • easy to train • white flowers • red berries

Pyracanthas resemble cotoneasters in many respects except that they have sharp thorns. The species *Pyracantha angustifolia* is an evergreen shrub, often used for hedging in the garden. It produces clusters of lovely white, five-petalled flowers in early summer, and these are followed by bright red berries in autumn. It easily develops a thick trunk and is an excellent subject for bonsai, being used for most styles.

Where to keep them

This species, originally from western China, is not reliably hardy (zones 6–8) and will require protection from hard frosts in winter. Keep your plants in an unheated greenhouse, or a heated greenhouse if the temperature is likely to fall below -5°C (23°F).

Pyracantha will lose its leaves in very cold weather. These plants enjoy full sun throughout the growing season.

How to look after them

Repotting: Repot pyracanthas in early spring. They are vigorous plants and should be repotted every other year. Use a free-draining compost consisting of two parts loam, one part peat (or garden compost) and one part sharp sand.

Pruning and pinching: Prune back the new shoots that grow after flowering in midsummer. Trim again before the winter, removing dead shoots and pruning out a few of the old flowering shoots to encourage new lateral shoots to develop. Take care not to remove all of the next year's buds. These are thorny shrubs and need to be pruned with scissors to maintain the overall shape of the tree rather than pinched with fingers.

Wiring: Pyracanthas are best wired in late autumn or early spring. The wires can be left on for one year.

Watering: Like other evergreen plants, pyracanthas need to be watered throughout the year. This includes dry spells in winter, although they need more water

Above: Pyracantha flowers profusely in late spring, and the flowers are followed by an abundance of brightly coloured berries in autumn.

Pyracantha angustifolia

in summer than in winter. Do not let the tree dry out during summer as this will make the leaves wither and fall.

Feeding: Start feeding only after flowering. Begin with one application of a high-nitrogen fertilizer in midsummer, followed by a low-nitrogen feed given in late summer.

Be aware! Coral spot and scab may cause problems, but fireblight, which affects members of the Rosaceae family, is the most serious problem. Infected shoots must be removed and burned and you should disinfect your secateurs. Aphids can be picked off by hand, removed with a jet of water or treated with a systemic insecticide if the infestation persists. Caterpillars are best removed by hand.

Rhododendron indicum

Satsuki azalea

half-hardy • evergreen • easy to keep and train • range of flower colours

The Satsuki azaleas, which have been developed from *Rhododendron simsii* and *R. indicum*, are probably the most popular flowering bonsai in Japan, and there are specialist societies dedicated to the plant. Satsukis flower in the fifth month of the oriental calendar (early June in Japan), and the flowers can last for up to a month. The flowers are showy and distinctive and are often multicoloured on the same plant. A Satsuki azalea in full bloom is a wonderful sight. These plants are usually trained in the informal upright style. They are readily available from bonsai nurseries.

Where to keep them

Satsuki azaleas are hardy in mild temperate climates (zones 6–8), where they do not need winter protection. They will withstand temperatures as low as -7°C (19°F) for short periods and an open shade structure is adequate protection. Where temperatures fall below -7°C (19°F) for prolonged periods, protection in an unheated or moderately heated greenhouse is advisable. During the growing season, they can be kept in full sun or semi-shade; the latter will result in better leaf colour.

Above: Many satsukis bear flowers of more than one colour on the same tree. Identifying a particular variety correctly can be difficult as many are very similar.

How to look after them

Repotting: Satsukis should be repotted every three or four years. Japanese growers repot immediately after flowering (late June in Japan), at the start of the rainy season. In temperate countries repotting in early spring, before flowering, is a better option. Use Japanese Kanuma soil, with 30 per cent sphagnum moss.

Pruning and pinching: Japanese growers sometimes prune hard in early spring, sacrificing the season's crop of flowers to produce better ramification and correct any faults in the tree. Deadhead immediately after the flowers have finished blooming.

Pruning can also be done at this time, before the leaves have hardened. Cut back laterals (secondary shoots) to two pairs of leaves. When you repot, prune away any dead or overcrowded branches. Satsuki azaleas are not usually pinched.

Wiring: Wiring is best left until autumn or winter. The wires can be left on for one year.

Watering: Water regularly and generously throughout the year, but especially when the plants are in bloom. The petals are easily damaged, so take care that you do not accidentally splash them with water. Japanese growers keep their Satsuki azaleas under cover when they are in flower to protect the blooms. Keep the compost just moist in winter.

Feeding: Apply a fairly weak fertilizer immediately after flowering and again in autumn. Japanese growers like to use rapeseed fertilizer.

Be aware! Vine weevils can be a serious problem. Check for the presence of the larvae when you are repotting. Kill any that you find and water nematodes into the soil in late spring. Leaf hoppers and rhododendron bugs can be treated with a spray of an appropriate insecticide. Foliage affected by azalea leaf gall should be picked off and burned. Aphids sometimes cluster on young shoots but can usually be removed by hand. A systemic insecticide can be applied if the infestation persists.

Unless the correct soil is used, satsukis will not grow well.

Satsuki azalea 'Hikari-no-tsukasa'

Stewartia, stuartia

hardy • deciduous • easy to keep • white/creamy flowers • attractive bark

Stewartias are closely related to camellias, and there are some evergreen species in the genus. However, the species used for bonsai, *Stewartia monadelpha* and *S. psuedocamellia* (Japanese stewartia, Hime Shara), are both deciduous. They have pointed, oval leaves and attractively mottled cinnamon-coloured bark. The cup-shaped flowers are white or creamy-white. These plants are usually grown in the informal style. They are popular subjects for bonsai, and good examples can usually be found in bonsai nurseries.

Where to keep them

S. monadelpha is native to Korea and southern Japan and is hardy in temperate areas (zone 6). *S. pseudocamellia* comes from Japan and is also hardy (zone 5). However, both species should be protected in a frost-free greenhouse or shed in prolonged periods of freezing weather in winter and early spring. In summer they can be kept in full sun, but when the flowers appear they should be shaded to prevent the flowers being scorched.

How to look after them

Repotting: Repot stewartias every two to three years, in early spring. Use a lime-free soil consisting of one part loam, one part Kanuma (or sphagnum moss peat) and one part sharp sand. Stewartias will not thrive in alkaline compost.

Pruning and pinching: Prune stewartias immediately after flowering, but be careful not to prune the shoots that are produced during the growing season because these carry next year's flowers. Lightly prune or pinch out the tips of the growing shoots at the end of summer in order to maintain the overall shape of the tree. If the branches become too congested, some of the inner twigs can be removed to allow air and light to penetrate and create a better structure.

Wiring: Wiring should be done in midsummer. Leave the wires on for no longer than one year.

Above: Stewartia flowers in midsummer. The loose petals and prominent stamens resemble those of the single-flowered camellias.

Watering: Water regularly throughout the growing season, increasing the amount of water in summer. In winter keep the compost just moist.

Feeding: Immediately after flowering, apply a high-nitrogen fertilizer. This should be supplemented in late summer with a low-nitrogen fertilizer.

Be aware! Vine weevils can be a serious problem for this species. Check for the larvae when you are repotting. If you find any, remove and kill them, and then water nematodes into the compost in late spring. Aphids sometimes cluster on new shoots but can usually be removed by hand. A systemic insecticide can be applied if the problem persists.

Stewartia monadelpha

Styrax japonica

Japanese snowbell

hardy • deciduous • easy to train • bell-shaped flowers • unusual fruit

This beautiful flowering tree makes a fine bonsai. It has glossy, dark green leaves, which turn yellow or red in autumn. Dainty, bell-shaped, pinkish-white flowers, borne in early summer, are followed by tiny aubergine-shaped fruits. These plants are easy to train as bonsai and are suitable for most styles. Although they are seen only occasionally in general plant nurseries, they are usually available from good bonsai specialists.

Above: The dainty and delicate styrax flowers are soon followed by tiny, aubergine-shaped fruits which last well into the autumn.

Where to keep them

This is a hardy species (zones 5–7), which is native to China, Korea and Japan. It requires no special protection in winter and can be kept in full sun throughout the growing season.

How to look after them

Repotting: Repot young plants every other year and older plants every three or four years. The best time to repot this species is in early spring. Japanese snowbells do best in well-drained, fertile, loamy soil, and Akadama soil with some additional organic material is ideal. They prefer neutral to acidic conditions.

Pruning and pinching: Prune Japanese snowbells lightly in midsummer and prune to shape in the spring. The flowers are borne on the current season's shoots, so there is no danger of losing flowers from spring pruning. To keep the tree looking neat, pinch out growing tips of new shoots as two or three leaves emerge, but take care not to remove the flower buds.

Wiring: Wiring is best done in winter or early spring. The wire should be left on for no more than one year.

Watering: Water regularly during the growing season, especially in summer. If the compost dries out completely, the leaves will shrivel. Keep the compost just moist in winter.

Feeding: Just after flowering, apply a high-nitrogen fertilizer. This should be followed by a low-nitrogen fertilizer in late summer.

Be aware! Japanese snowbells are generally trouble free, and as long as you water regularly

they should live for many years. Branches on older trees sometimes suffer from die-back. If this happens, cut back to healthy tissue and the stem will reshoot the following year.

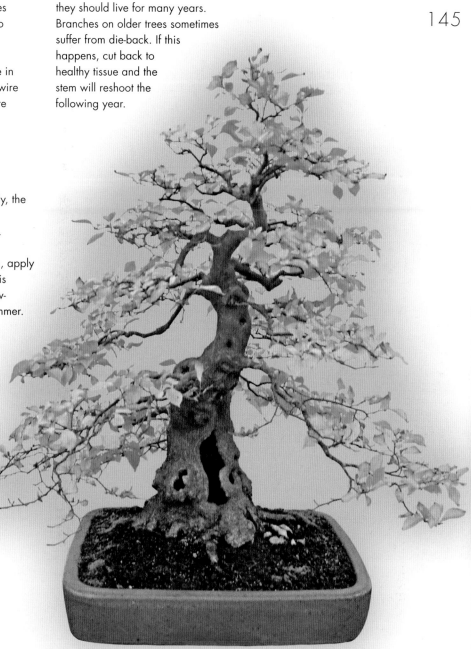

Styrax japonica

Wisteria

hardy • deciduous • more challenging • scented racemes in a range of colours

outdoor flowering bonsai

Wisterias are the most beautiful of climbing plants, and the long, scented racemes of blue, purple, pink or white flowers look quite stunning. *Wisteria floribunda* (Japanese wisteria, Fuji) and *W. sinensis* (Chinese wisteria) can both be trained as bonsai, and keeping the plants alive is not difficult. Getting them to flower year after year can be a challenge, however. Wisteria bonsai are still produced in large numbers in Japan for both the home and export markets. They are widely available in bonsai nurseries, and large specimens are much sought after by enthusiasts.

Most wisterias are deliciously scented, and that is one of their attractions as bonsai, but the Chinese wisteria is the most fragrant of all. The fragrence of the white varieties is very strong.

Where to keep them
Wisterias are hardy plants (zone 6) and do not require special protection in winter. They do best if kept in full sun throughout the growing season.

How to look after them
Repotting: Wisterias should be repotted every other year into a free-draining, loam-based compost. Akadama soil mixed with a little sharp sand is ideal. The best time of year to repot wisterias is either in early spring or immediately after flowering.

Pruning and pinching: Prune back long tendrils to three buds in late summer. Branches that are too long should also be cut back at

Above: Wisteria floribunda 'Violacea Plena', one of the rare forms of Japanese wisteria with double mauve flowers.

the same time. Do not prune in early spring or after late summer as this will remove the potential flower buds. The growing tips of new wisteria shoots are not pinched out, as this will simply encourage the growth of lots of weak laterals that do not set flower buds.

Wiring: Pruning is sufficient to train wisterias and they do not require any wiring.

Watering: Wisterias need a lot of water throughout the growing season, especially when they are flowering, and in midsummer. Some growers suggest standing the plant in a bowl of water at the height of summer, but leaving plants with their roots permanently in water for months on end will lead to root rot and possibly the death of the plant. It is better to stand the plant in a shallow bowl of water for no more than three or four hours on very hot days or simply water heavily several times a day in warm, dry weather. This should prevent the leaves from wilting. In winter keep the compost just moist.

Feeding: Apply a high-nitrogen fertilizer immediately after flowering. Feed again in late summer with a low-nitrogen fertilizer. Japanese rapeseed fertilizer is particularly beneficial for wisterias. A large handful on each pot after flowering should ensure repeat flowering.

Be aware! Scale insects can be a problem. Treat with a systemic insecticide. Wisterias are otherwise trouble free.

Wisteria floribunda 'Kuchi beni'

indoor
bonsai

Indoor bonsai

Indoor bonsai are a fairly recent development, introduced some fifty years ago to meet the demand for bonsai that could be grown successfully inside the home. Like houseplants, indoor bonsai tend to be tropical and subtropical species that will survive in homes in Europe and North America. Some Mediterranean and a few temperate species can also be adapted to grow indoors.

Care of indoor bonsai

People who have been growing bonsai for many years seldom keep indoor varieties, largely because they are grown in an unnatural environment and, in consequence, their potential is limited. Outdoor bonsai are more likely to thrive, and there are more species to choose from. However, although indoor bonsai are slightly more difficult to manage, mastering their care is within the reach of everyone.

Left: Most varieties of *Ficus* make good indoor bonsai. This is *Ficus microcarpa*.

The secret lies in selecting species that are easy to keep and in using simple growing aids to provide the conditions in which they can do well. Plants generally do not grow well indoors because there is insufficient light, humidity and fresh air. If these requirements can be met by artificial means, the plants will thrive. For example, improving light levels by placing a fluorescent lamp above the bonsai will make a world of difference. Similarly, humidity and warmth can be improved by standing the bonsai in a drip tray containing gravel or pebbles and by controlling the room temperature to suit the species.

Indoor species

There are a number of species that make reliable houseplants, and these are ideal for indoor bonsai too. The indoor bonsai described in this section are those that have been grown successfully in the West for many years. They are also popular species, which means they are fairly easy to obtain. The selection is by no means comprehensive. It is possible to use ordinary houseplants as material for creating your own bonsai, by simply transplanting them into bonsai containers and then shaping and pruning them. A good bonsai nursery should be able to give you sound advice on how to go about progressing in the hobby.

Above: Serissa's variegated leaves are as attractive as its flowers.

By far the most common indoor bonsai sold in Europe and North America is *Ulmus parvifolia* (Chinese elm; see pages 188–189). This is also one of the easiest and most reliable plants for beginners. It is a hardy species and can withstand a wide range of conditions, and it is one of the few species that can be grown as both an indoor and an outdoor bonsai.

Carmona microphylla (Fukien tea; see pages 154–155) and *Serissa foetida* (see pages 186–187) are also widely available, but they can be difficult for newcomers to bonsai, and do not make ideal 'starter' plants. Unless you can provide additional lighting and humidity, they will struggle in the average home.

Many species of *Ficus* (fig; see pages 164–167), which are often grown as houseplants, make excellent and easy-to-grow indoor

Above: Bougainvillea offers a multitude of bright flower colours.

bonsai. This is a huge genus and there are dozens of species to choose from, but among the best are *Ficus benjamina*, *F. microcarpa* and *F. neriifolia*.

If you enjoy experimenting with plants, try growing other tropical and semi-tropical species and see how you get on. The range is enormous, and the following are just a few of those that have been used successfully by enthusiasts in various parts of the world and that are worth trying: *Adenium* (desert rose), *Bambusa ventricosa* (Buddha's belly bamboo), *Beaucarnea* (syn. *Nolina*), *Calliandra* (powder-puff tree), *Cassia*, *Cuphea*, *Cycas* (sago palm), *Euphorbia pulcherrima* (poinsettia), *Fortunella* (kumquat; see also pages 158–159), *Ixora*, *Hibiscus*, *Jacaranda*, *Lantana*, *Myrtus* (myrtle) and *Nandina domestica* (heavenly bamboo).

Bougainvillea

tender • evergreen • challenging • range of colours • good for driftwood

indoor bonsai

Most of the bougainvilleas available today are cultivars of *Bougainvillea glabra*, *B. spectablis* and *B. x buttiana*, and they have been developed to provide a wide range of colourful bracts in shades of red, pink, mauve, yellow, orange and white. The bracts (often mistaken for flowers) are borne on the current year's growth of the thorny stems of these evergreen climbers. They are popular outdoor bonsai in southern and Southeast Asia, but must be kept indoors in cool temperate regions. They are best grown in the informal upright style, and are very suitable for carving to create a hollow-trunk driftwood effect.

Where to keep them

Bougainvilleas thrive in hot, sunny, dry conditions and are found mainly in tropical, subtropical and Mediterranean regions. *B. glabra*, *B. spectabilis* and *B. buttiana* originated in Brazil, and even though *B. buttiana* is slightly less tender, none of these plants will survive a winter outdoors in temperate areas (zones 10–11). The long flowering season occurs mainly in the cooler winter months, but they will not bloom well if kept outdoors in areas with excessive rainfall. Nevertheless, given the right conditions your bonsai will produce bracts.

These plants love a warm, sunny position with a minimum temperature of 5°C (41°F); ideally, the winter temperature should be 8–15°C (46–59°F). They cannot tolerate frost. When bougainvilleas are grown as indoor bonsai they must be kept in a warm, sunny room or a heated conservatory. If you do not have such conditions

Above: The yellow form of bougainvillea is rare, but it is no more difficult to care for than the common mauve variety.

you will have to provide supplementary heating and lighting, otherwise they will simply languish and die.

How to look after them

Repotting: Bougainvilleas do best when they are potbound, so you should repot plants only every three or four years. Repotting should be done in late spring. Use a loam-based, free-draining compost for bougainvillea.

Pruning and pinching: Immediately after flowering, prune back hard to the old wood to encourage new shoots to grow. The colourful bracts are carried on the current season's wood. Do not keep on

pruning or pinching out the new growth or you will have no bracts for the next year. If you want to carve the thick trunks to resemble the hollow trunks found in nature, do so in spring and summer when cuts heal quickly.

Wiring: Wiring should not be necessary because the shaping is achieved mainly through pruning.

Watering: Do not overwater your bougainvillea but at the same time never let the rootball dry out so much that the leaves go limp. During winter, allow the surface of the compost to dry slightly before you water. In spring, when the buds begin to develop, increase the amount of water so that the compost remains just moist, but never saturated. Misting is advisable if the room's atmosphere is very dry.

Feeding: Apply an organic fertilizer or a low-nitrogen fertilizer during the growing season to promote flowering. A specially formulated rose or tomato fertilizer is ideal.

Be aware! Bougainvilleas are susceptible to all the insect pests that occur under glass: aphids, scale insects and red spider mites. Aphids can sometimes be picked off by hand and misting will help control red spider mites, but severe

infestations of sap-sucking insects are best controlled by systemic insecticides. Bougainvilleas do not respond well to being moved to

different positions. Allow your plants several weeks to acclimatize to new conditions after you have moved them.

Bougainvillea

Carmona microphylla

Fukien tea

tender • evergreen • challenging • scented flowers

This shrub, which is also known as *Carmona retusa* and formerly as *Ehretia buxifolia*, is now grown extensively throughout Asia. It has glossy, dark green leaves and delicate, slightly scented white flowers. The greyish bark is fissured. The species stands up to pruning well, which makes it particularly suitable for bonsai. It can be trained into most styles, particularly informal upright. It is widely available in bonsai nurseries, but it is not an easy plant and should not be taken on by newcomers to the hobby.

Where to keep them

Fukien tea is native to China, Japan, Korea and Taiwan, but it is not hardy in temperate areas (zone 10). Plants require warm, humid and bright conditions to do well, and if you cannot provide these conditions your bonsai will struggle to survive. A windowsill in a warm, bright kitchen or living room could be suitable, but make sure that the temperature never falls below 10°C (50°F) and that there are no sudden and wide temperature swings. Do not stand plants in draughts. Plants will benefit from standing outside on warm, sunny days in summer.

How to look after them

Repotting: Repot your Fukien tea every two or three years, but only when the rootball is potbound. Repot in late spring. Use a fertile compost consisting of two parts leaf mould, one part loam and one part sharp sand.

Pruning and pinching: Prune sparingly and only to maintain the shape. This species flowers on the current season's wood, so take care that you do not remove new growth unless it is spoiling the shape of the tree. Prune in late winter or early spring, before the plant starts into growth. Pinch back the growing tips of laterals (secondary branches) to two or three leaves as soon as they have borne six or seven leaves. Continue to do this throughout the growing season.

Wiring: Although shaping of Fukien tea is mostly achieved through pruning, stems can be wired at any time of the year for no more than eight weeks.

Watering: These plants like humid conditions, but water carefully so that the compost never becomes

Above: Fukien tea (*Carmona microphylla*) has bright white flowers with a light scent, which appear at the ends of stems like stars.

waterlogged. Keep the compost moist at all times, but in winter allow the surface to dry a little before watering. Plants will appreciate regular misting to maintain a humid atmosphere.

Feeding: Apply a high-nitrogen fertilizer in spring. In late summer, plants will benefit from a low-nitrogen fertilizer.

Be aware! This is a temperamental species and extremely difficult to grow as an indoor bonsai in temperate countries, although it does well in Mediterranean and subtropical climates. The leaves sometimes turn yellow and drop, which signifies too much water.

Carmona microphylla

Celtis sinensis

Chinese hackberry, Japanese hackberry

hardy • deciduous • easy to keep • orange fruits

There are about 70 species in this genus, which belongs to the same family as elms. Some are hardy and grow in northern temperate regions, while others are found in tropical Asia. They have an upright habit of growth, attractive bark and they bear small, glossy, dark green leaves, small green flowers in spring and small orange fruits that ripen to reddish-brown. These plants are especially suitable for informal and formal upright bonsai styles. *Celtis sinensis* is very popular in China, from where large numbers of plants are exported to the West for use as indoor bonsai.

Where to keep them

Chinese hackberry, which is native to eastern China, Korea and Japan, is fully hardy in temperate areas (zones 6–9) and can be kept outdoors where winter temperatures do not fall below -5°C (23°F). However, the plants imported as bonsai from China should be treated as indoor plants. They need maximum light to grow well and will do best on a bright, sunny windowsill. They should be turned regularly so that they do not 'lean' towards the light source. In summer, like many other indoor bonsai, Chinese hackberry plants will benefit from standing outside in a sunny position.

In winter, when the tree has shed its leaves, it is better to keep a Chinese hackberry in a cool room, ideally no warmer than 8°C (46°F), so that it remains dormant and will come into leaf and flower the following year. Trees that are kept in conditions that encourage them to grow all year round quickly exhaust themselves and eventually die.

How to look after them

Repotting: You should repot Chinese hackberries every two or three years in early spring. Use a fertile, free-draining compost, consisting of two parts loam and one part sharp sand.

Pruning and pinching: To maintain the shape, prune this species at any time between spring and the

Above: The glossy leaves of the Chinese hackberry look fresh throughout the summer. In autumn, they turn yellow and fall.

end of summer. Cut back over-long branches and pinch out new shoots that have three or four buds, pinching back to one or two buds.

Wiring: You can apply wires from spring to autumn if necessary, although most shaping is achieved by pruning.

Watering: This species should be watered regularly and generously during the growing season, watering as soon as the surface of the compost feels dry. In winter keep the compost just moist. This species will not survive in waterlogged compost. Misting is advisable if the room's atmosphere is very dry.

Feeding: During the growing season apply a weak solution of liquid fertilizer once a fortnight. Stop feeding at the end of summer.

Be aware! Like many other indoor bonsai, these plants are sometimes infested with aphids and red spider mites. Aphids can sometimes be picked off by hand and misting will help control red spider mites. If your plants are standing outside for the summer, jetting water at the affected shoots will often dislodge the insects. If the problem persists, apply a systemic insecticide. They are otherwise trouble-free plants.

Celtis sinensis

Citrus

Orange, lemon

tender • evergreen • fragrant white flowers • yellow or orange fruits

indoor bonsai

These familiar plants make attractive, easy-to-keep bonsai. The mid to pale green leaves are oval and borne on often spiny stems. The fragrant white flowers appear from late spring to summer and are followed by the yellow or orange fruits. Also included in this group is *Fortunella hindsii* (dwarf kumquat), which is similar to citrus but bears golden-yellow fruits. The plants are usually grown in the informal upright and broom styles. They are very common in Asia – especially around the lunar New Year in China where fruits symbolize wealth – but harder to get hold of in Europe and North America.

Where to keep them

All these plants are native to Mediterranean or subtropical areas and they are tender in temperate areas (zone 10). They should be kept indoors, in good light, when temperatures fall below 3–5°C (37–41°F). In summer they can stand outside in a sunny, sheltered position.

How to look after them

Repotting: Repot these plants only when the roots are potbound, which may not be more often than every three years. Repot in late winter to early spring, using a moisture-retentive, free-draining compost. All these species prefer neutral to acidic conditions.

Above: Citrus bonsai are grown for their fragrant blossom and beautiful fruit. The fruit remain on the tree for a long time.

Pruning and pinching: Light pruning only is required for established indoor citrus bonsai. Trimming with scissors or pinching out of the growing tips will maintain the shape of the bonsai and encourage a fine ramification.

Pruning and pinching can be done in spring and summer, but be careful not to remove the flowering buds in the process. Thin out the twigs if the structure becomes too dense. Remove any fruits from the plant at the end of winter.

Wiring: Only wire when creating structure. Wire in late spring, leaving the wires on for a year.

Watering: Water citrus plants freely in summer, making sure that the compost never dries out. At the same time, make sure that the rootball is never in waterlogged soil. These plants prefer to be kept drier in winter, in just moist compost. Misting is advisable if the room's atmosphere is very dry.

Feeding: Feed these plants in summer only (not spring), after flowering and when the fruits have set. If you give plants too much fertilizer, the leaves will turn yellow and drop.

Be aware! Overwatering and overfeeding can lead to leaf drop. Scale insects can be a problem and should be treated with a systemic insecticide.

Citrus fortunella

160 Crassula

tender • succulent • easy to keep • attractive shape

Two species from this large genus of succulent plants – *Crassula arborescens* (silver jade plant) and *C. ovata* (syn. *C. portulacaria*; jade plant, dollar plant) – are particularly suitable for bonsai. They develop a tree-like habit with sturdy trunks and recognizable branches. *C. ovata* has the added advantage of small leaves, and a trunk and branches that can be wired into any shape. This species is used extensively for bonsai in India and South Africa because they can be made into bonsai of all styles and sizes from *mame* (mini-bonsai) to very large specimens.

Above: The small-leaved crassulas, such as this *Crassula ovata*, make excellent tree-like bonsai, even though they are succulent plants.

Where to keep them

Both *Crassula arborescens* and *C. ovata* are native to southern Africa and should be regarded as tender plants (zone 10). They can withstand minimum temperatures of 5–7°C (41–45°F). When crassulas are grown as indoor bonsai they should be kept in a bright position, although direct sunlight is not strictly necessary for them to flourish.

How to look after them

Repotting: When grown in an indoor environment, crassulas can be left in the same pot for as long as four or five years. In fact, repotting too frequently will result in long internodes and large leaves. The best time of year to repot these plants is during late spring. They must be repotted into a free-draining compost, such as one of the proprietary cactus mixes. Alternatively, try a compost consisting of equal parts of loam, leaf mould and sharp sand.

Pruning and pinching: Maintain the shape of crassula bonsai during the growing season by trimming new shoots with scissors or pinching out the growing tips, pruning back to two or three pairs of leaves. This will encourage a fine branch ramification. Hard pruning of indoor crassula is required only if you wish to change the structure of the tree.

Wiring: *C. ovata* has pliable branches that can be easily wired into any shape. The wires may be applied at any time of year, and they should be left on for about one year. *C. arborescens* does not respond well to wiring and this species should be shaped by pruning alone.

Watering: Crassulas prefer fairly dry conditions, so water sparingly in summer and give them even less in winter. Overwatering will cause the leaves of these species to grow large and floppy, making the tree top heavy and unstable, or leading to root rot.

Feeding: Feed crassulas once a month in summer, using a low-nitrogen fertilizer.

Be aware! Scale insects can be a problem for this tree and should be treated with a weak dose of systemic insecticide. Aphids can usually be removed by hand, but if the infestation persists treat them with a systemic insecticide. Because crassulas are not repotted every year, vine weevils can be a problem. Water nematodes into the compost in late spring. Otherwise, the plants are usually trouble free.

Crassula ovata

Eugenia

tender • evergreen • easy • attractive foliage • white flowers • colourful fruit

This is a large genus, belonging to the Myrtaceae family, of which two species – *Eugenia brasilensis* (Brazil cherry) and *E. uniflora* (Surinam cherry, pitanga) – are suitable for growing as bonsai. They have glossy, ovate leaves, which are tinged with bronze when they first emerge in spring. Clusters of fragrant white flowers are followed by colourful, edible fruits, although plants can be difficult to get to fruit when they are grown as indoor bonsai. They are mainly grown in the informal upright style and are widely available from bonsai nurseries.

Above: Eugenias have glossy green leaves and bark that flakes as the tree matures, adding interest to the trunk.

You should aim to provide a minimum temperature of 15–18°C (59–65°F) with little fluctuation.

How to look after them

Repotting: Repot eugenias every two or three years. The best time of year to do this is in spring, before the new leaves emerge. A proprietary bonsai mix, such as Kanuma, is suitable. Alternatively, use a fertile, free-draining, loam-based compost on the acidic side of neutral.

Pruning and pinching: Light pruning only is required for eugenias grown indoors, in order to maintain the shape of your bonsai. Prune and pinch out the tips of new shoots during the growing season, pruning back to two or three new leaves.

Wiring: Although most shaping is achieved through pruning, branches can be wired. This should be done during

Where to keep them

Both these species of eugenia are native to Brazil and are tender (zone 10). They should be kept in as bright a position as possible and somewhere that is warm and free from draughts. A sunny windowsill is suitable, but make sure that the temperature does not drop at night. Although both species are evergreen, they will lose their leaves if it gets too cold.

midsummer, when the stems have hardened. The wires can be left on for about a year.

Watering: Do not overwater. Water sparingly in winter. Increase the amount of water you give in spring and summer but allow the surface of the compost to dry between waterings.

Feeding: A general fertilizer should be applied once a month from spring to autumn.

Be aware! Eugenias grown as bonsai rarely produce the colourful fruits for which the species are grown in gardens. Apart from needing a constantly warm environment, these species are relatively trouble free.

Eugenia uniflora

Fig

tender • evergreen • easy to keep • very diverse

This large genus of mostly evergreen shrubs and trees is found in tropical and subtropical areas throughout world. Many of the species have distinctive aerial roots, which grow from the trunk and branches. They make excellent houseplants and are therefore also good as indoor bonsai in temperate countries. They are among the most popular genera for bonsai, and large numbers are produced in China for the West, where they are available through the internet and in shops and bonsai centres.

The species are incredibly diverse, but the most popular and suitable species for bonsai are *Ficus benjamina*, *F. microcarpa* and *F. neriifolia*, which are discussed here. The care of other species is summarized on pages 166–167.

Where to keep them

F. benjamina (weeping fig), *F. microcarpa* (syn. *F. retusa*; Indian laurel) and *F. neriifolia* are tender plants (zones 10–11) and will grow best at temperatures of 20–28°C (68–82°F), although they will tolerate temperatures of 13–15°C (55–59°F) for short periods. They prefer a bright position in direct sunlight, but will also grow reasonably well in shade, especially *F. benjamina* and *F. microcarpa*. Keep them out of draughts. In summer they can stand outside in a sunny position.

How to look after them

Repotting: Figs should be repotted every two or three years. Although these trees can be repotted at any

Above: Ficus microcarpa has lovely small leaves. It is also a very compact plant, which is why it is one of the most popular ficuses for indoor bonsai.

time of the year, it is best to do this in spring. Use a compost consisting of equal parts of peat (or garden compost), sharp sand and loam.

Pruning and pinching: Hard pruning is not usually required in indoor environments. Keep the tree in shape during the growing season by trimming new shoots or pinching out the growing tips, pruning back to two or three

leaves. They may also benefit from leaf pruning (partial or total defoliation, see page 195) in early summer. All will exude a white milky sap when cut, but there is no need to apply paste to the wounds because the sap will stop naturally.

Wiring: You can wire these plants at any time of the year. Remove the wires as soon as the tree has set, which may be only a few months.

Watering: Keep the compost damp, but never waterlogged, by watering regularly but sparingly, although you can increase the amount of water slightly in summer. Most species of *Ficus* appreciate having their foliage misted from time to time, which also encourages aerial roots to form.

Feeding: Unusually, you can feed these plants throughout the year. Apply a general fertilizer every two to three weeks throughout the growing season and reduce this to once a month in winter.

Be aware! These three species of *Ficus* are among the easiest to care for, but they can still be temperamental. They will lose their leaves if conditions change – if you move them to another position or when you bring them home from the shop, for example – or if you underwater or overwater. They will produce new leaves quickly, however, so do not worry.

All the species in the genus are susceptible to scale insects, which can be found clustering on the stems and undersides of the leaves. To remove them, apply a weak dose of a systemic insecticide.

Ficus microcarpa 'Green Island'

Fig – other species and cultivars

tender • evergreen/deciduous • more challenging • interesting

The following fig varieties have slightly different growth habits and are more challenging, but reliable none the less. The care instructions apply to *Ficus aurea*, *F. buxifolia* (box-leaved fig), *F. pelkan*, *F. religiosa* (bo tree, peepul), *F. bengalensis* (banyan), *F. rumphii*, *F. rubignosa* (Port Jackson fig), *F. Burt-davii* (a miniature fig), *F. infectoria* (grey fig) and *F. virens*. *F. carica* (edible fig) could also be included in this category of indoor bonsai, although it is a hardy species that is best kept outdoors, with slight protection in winter.

Unfortunately, some of these species may not be easily available in Europe and North America. Specialist ficus growers and bonsai enthusiasts in India, Indonesia, Thailand, Phillipines and Hawii have fine specimens.

Where to keep them
These ficuses prefer slightly warmer and brighter conditions to those listed on pages 164–165, ranging from 19–30°C (66–85°F). They can be placed near a radiator in winter, provided the soil is not allowed to dry out. They also grow better under artificial lighting. Keep them out of draughts. In summer they can stand outside in a sunny position.

How to look after them
Repotting: Repot ficuses in late spring every two or three years, when the tree has become potbound. Use a compost of equal parts of peat (or garden compost), sharp sand and loam.

Pruning and pinching: Hard pruning is not usually required for ficuses in indoor environments, but can be done at the same time as repotting. Keep the tree in shape during the growing season by trimming new shoots or pinching out the growing tips, pruning back to two or three leaves. They may also benefit from leaf pruning (partial or total defoliation, see page 195) in early summer. The white milky sap is self-sealing and will stop after a while.

Above: Most figs have impressive root buttresses like this one. In time they fuse together to form a matted plate.

Wiring: You can wire these plants at any time of the year. Remove the wires as soon as the tree has set, which may be only a few months.

Watering: Keep the soil damp, but never waterlogged. Increase the amount of water slightly in summer. Most species appreciate having their foliage misted from time to time, which also encourages the formation of aerial roots.

Feeding: Unusually, you can feed these plants throughout the year. Apply a general fertilizer every two to three weeks throughout the growing season and reduce this to once a month in winter.

Be aware! *Ficus* can be temperamental, losing their leaves if conditions change or if you underwater or overwater. However, they will produce new leaves quickly. All the species in this genus are susceptible to scale insects. This can be treated with a weak dose of a systemic insecticide.

Ficus rumphii

Fuchsia

tender or half-hardy • deciduous/evergreen • easy to keep • range of colours

The hundred or so species in this genus have been hybridized to produce more than 8,000 cultivars, and it is possible to find the colourful and distinctive flowers in every imaginable shade of pink, red, purple and orange as well as white. The tender and half-hardy plants make excellent indoor bonsai, especially those that have tiny leaves and flowers, and they are suitable for small and mini-bonsai. Fuchsias are not usually seen in bonsai nurseries because this group of plants tends to be grown only by amateur enthusiasts.

Where to keep them

Fuchsias are native to mountainous areas of New Zealand and Central and South America, and although some species and cultivars are hardy, most are tender or, at best, half-hardy (zones 6–10). They will do best in a bright position, such as on a windowsill, especially during the growing season. When the plant is dormant in winter, light is not as important. Tender fuchsias require a warm environment, with a temperature of 15–20°C (59–68°C). Hardy and half-hardy plants can be kept in cooler conditions, at 5–15°C (41–59°F). Fuchsias kept in temperatures above 4–5°C (40–41°F) all year round will remain evergreen.

Above: The dangling flowers of fuchsia are immediately recognizable. Cultivars with small leaves and tiny flowers are ideal for bonsai.

How to look after them

Repotting: Fuchsias are vigorous plants and need to be repotted each year, from early to late spring, or when the plant is potbound. They also need a fertile, moisture-retentive but free-draining compost containing plenty of organic matter. Use a mixture consisting of three parts peat (or garden compost), one part loam and one part sharp sand. If possible, add some leaf mould to the compost.

Pruning and pinching: As fuchsias flower on the current season's shoots, pruning should be done in early spring. After the first flowering, the flowers should be deadheaded and the plant lightly pruned again. Most fuchsias will produce two crops of flowers in a year. If pinching out new shoots to maintain the shape, be sure not to remove too many flower buds.

Wiring: Fuchsias have soft stems and should not be wired.

Watering: Make sure that fuchsias do not dry out. Water regularly throughout the growing season and keep the compost just moist in winter. Misting is advisable if the room's atmosphere is very dry.

Feeding: Fuchsias are hungry feeders. During the growing season, apply a liquid feed of a high-nitrogen fertiliser every fortnight. When they are in flower, switch to a low-nitrogen fertilizer. These plants will also benefit from foliar feeds from time to time. Stop feeding by late summer.

Be aware! Fuchsias require plenty of attention in summer, when they grow rapidly and flower. They are far less demanding in autumn and winter when they need a period of dormancy. They are susceptible to aphid infestation from spring right through to late summer. Spray infested plants with a gentle insecticide. Mildew can also be a problem with plants that are not carefully watered. Remove and burn infected leaves and apply an appropriate fungicide.

Fuchsia reflexa

Gardenia jasminoides

Gardenia

tender • evergreen • easy to keep • attractive foliage • scented white flowers

This species of gardenia (sometimes known as _G. augusta_) has become a popular houseplant in recent years because of its beautiful white, scented flowers and glossy, dark green leaves. It is not surprising that it is also now used for indoor bonsai. A number of different cultivars are used, including some with small, variegated leaves. They are fairly easy to keep but will not flower profusely unless they are kept in a heated greenhouse. The informal upright style is the most suitable for these plants. They are widely available in North America and Asia; rarer in Europe.

Where to keep them

Gardenias, which originated in China, Taiwan and Japan, are tropical plants (zones 8–11), which need a minimum temperature of 10–15°C (50–59°F). They also need a bright position but should not stand in direct sunlight. Keep them away from draughts and cold. If you keep the plant on a windowsill, move it to a warmer position at night and when the curtains are drawn. In summer they can moved outside to stand in partial shade.

How to look after them

Repotting: Repot gardenias every two years in early spring. They need a lime-free (ericaceous) compost, which must be fertile and free-draining. Use a mix consisting of two parts loam, one part leaf mould and one part sharp sand.

Pruning and pinching: Hard pruning is required only if the plant has lost its shape or become

Above: The gardenias used for bonsai in Japan have small leaves and tiny flowers that set orange fruit if pollinated.

congested. Otherwise, prune after flowering to maintain a good overall shape. Avoid pruning in midsummer so you do not remove any of the flowering shoots. As soon as new laterals have produced six or seven leaves, pinch them back to three leaves.

Wiring: Wiring is not usually necessary for gardenia bonsai. However, if you want to shape one of the stems, wait until it has become woody and hard. Leave the wires on for no longer than one year.

Watering: Water gardenias regularly and freely during the growing season, reducing the amount of water in autumn and keeping the compost moist in winter. Make sure that the rootball never dries out. The foliage will benefit from regular misting.

Feeding: Apply a high-nitrogen fertilizer in spring and a low-nitrogen fertilizer in summer. Gardenia plants also appreciate being given a foliar feed in spring.

Be aware! Gardenias must have a fairly constant temperature to thrive. They are susceptible to sap-sucking pests, such as scale insect, aphids and whitefly. Treat them with a systemic insecticide if there are too many to pick off by hand. Mildew can also be a problem when there is little movement of air around the leaves. Remove and burn infected leaves, apply fungicide if necessary and water carefully.

Gardenia jasminoides

Ilex crenata

Japanese holly, box-leaved holly

hardy • evergreen • easy to keep • glossy foliage • black berries

This hardy, evergreen holly has glossy, dark green leaves with scalloped (not spiny) edges. In summer it produces small white flowers, and these are followed by black berries. Large numbers of bonsai are produced in China for the indoor bonsai market in the West. When they are grown indoors they are reliable and easy to keep as long as they are kept in a fairly cool position. The holly is most suited to the informal upright and cascade styles.

Where to keep them

Although Japanese holly is a hardy plant, native to Russia, Japan and Korea (zones 7–10), when it is grown as a bonsai it is regarded as an indoor subject. Keep plants in a bright location, such as a windowsill, and in summer they will benefit from a spell outdoors. In winter they prefer a room that is cool rather than one that is too warm so that they can undergo a period of dormancy.

How to look after them

Repotting: Japanese hollies should be repotted every other year. The best time of year to do this is during late spring. This species needs a moisture-retentive but free-draining mix, consisting of equal parts loam and leaf mould. You may need to add some sharp sand to improve the drainage.

Pruning and pinching: In early spring, after the new shoots have hardened, prune back the new growth to maintain the shape of your bonsai. If you want berries to form, do not prune away the shoots that bear the flowers in summer. Pinch out the growing tips of new shoots as necessary to keep the tree looking trim.

Wiring: If necessary, wiring can be done in early spring. Protect the stems with raffia because they can be brittle. Leave on the wiring for two years to allow the branches to set.

Above: The leaves of a healthy Japanese holly are shiny and oval, resembling the foliage of box.

Watering: Water regularly, increasing the amount of water when the flowers appear to encourage the formation of berries. Allow the surface of the compost to dry slightly between waterings. Keep the compost just moist in winter, but never allow it to dry out completely. Misting is advisable if the room's atmosphere is very dry.

Feeding: Apply a general fertilizer throughout the growing season.

Be aware! The young shoots of Japanese holly are sometimes infested with aphids, but these can usually be removed by hand or with a jet of water. Apply a systemic insecticide if the problem persists. Overwatering can sometimes lead to root rot, but otherwise these are trouble-free plants.

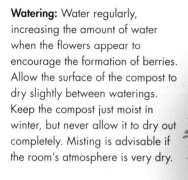

Ilex crenata

Privet

hardy • evergreen/deciduous • white flowers • blue-black berries

Ligustrum lucidum (Chinese privet) and *L. sinense* belong to the same genus as *L. vulgare* (see pages 88–89), which is grown as an outdoor bonsai. *L. lucidum* is an evergreen plant with small, glossy, dark green leaves, white flowers and blue-black berries. *L. sinense* is a deciduous species, with light green leaves, white flowers and purple-black berries. Both these species are fast growing and easy to train as bonsai (usually in the informal upright style), and vast numbers are exported from China for sale in Europe and North America.

Where to keep them

L. lucidum is native to China, Korea and Japan, while *L. sinense* came originally from China. Both are hardy plants (zones 7–11), and they can be grown outdoors, where they will do well. If they are grown as indoor subjects they need a bright, sunny but not too warm position, and both species will benefit from being moved outdoors in summer. Variegated forms show better coloration when they are kept in full sun.

Above: The leaves of the privet used for indoor bonsai are slightly rounded and a lighter shade of green than the common privet used for hedging.

How to look after them

Repotting: Repot both these species of privet every other year. The best time of year to repot is in mid to late spring. They need a free-draining compost, such as one consisting of two parts loam and one part sharp sand, but they are not fussy plants and will grow in almost any compost as long as it is not waterlogged.

Pruning and pinching: These species are less vigorous than *L. vulgare* (which is recommended as an outdoor plant, see pages 88–89), so need a lighter pruning, in midsummer, to maintain the plant's shape. Pinch out the growing tips of new shoots as necessary to keep the bonsai trim.

Wiring: Branches can be wired in summer. Remove the wires if they are biting deeply into the bark. Initial training wires can be left on for one or two years, while the branches set.

Watering: Water regularly but take care that you do not overwater. The compost should be kept moist all year round, but give more water in summer when plants are growing. Misting is advisable if the room's atmosphere is very dry.

Feeding: Feed both these species of privet with a general fertilizer once every two or three weeks during spring and summer.

Be aware! These privets are relatively trouble free, but they do best in fairly cool conditions. If they are kept in too warm a room, especially in winter, they will produce leggy shoots. They are susceptible to sap-sucking insects, such as scale insects, aphids and whitefly. Spray or apply a systemic insecticide if there are too many to pick off by hand. Branches sometimes die back for no apparent reason. If this happens, cut the affected stems back to healthy tissue.

Ligustrum sinense

Satin wood, jasmine orange, Chinese box

tender • evergreen • challenging • fragrant flowers • bright red berries

This attractive shrub or small tree has pinnate, glossy, dark green leaves and smooth grey bark. Strongly scented white flowers are borne in clusters – all year round where it is warm enough – and are followed by round, red berries. It is a difficult species to grow successfully as an indoor bonsai and cannot be recommended as a 'starter' plant. *Murraya paniculata* is suitable for any bonsai style except windswept. It is very common in Asia, but harder to find in Europe and North America.

Where to keep them

Satin wood is native to tropical areas of southeast Asia, China and India, and it is tender (zone 10). It must be kept in a bright, warm, humid and draught-free place with a minimum temperature of 18°C (65°F).

How to look after them

Repotting: Repot satin wood bonsai every second or third year in spring. They need a fertile but free-draining compost, consisting of two parts loam, one part peat (or garden compost) and one part sharp sand.

Pruning and pinching: Heavy pruning to shape the plant can be done in spring, and light pruning can be done throughout the growing season. Be careful not to prune out the flowering shoots. Cut or pinch back the shoots to two leaves as soon as five or six new leaves have emerged.

Above: Murraya leaves are a bright shiny green and highly aromatic. The wood of the tree is extremely dense and hard.

Wiring: Satin wood is grown extensively throughout Asia for the hardness of its wood, and woody branches are almost impossible to bend with wire, so any shaping must be done before the stems lignify. Young, semi-hard stems can be wired at any time, but do not leave the wire in place for more than eight weeks.

Watering: This species needs moisture all year round, and in winter the compost should be kept

moist. In summer, water before
the compost begins to dry out and
stand the pot on a tray of pebbles
or gravel to increase the humidity.
Mist the foliage regularly.

Feeding: Apply a general fertilizer
once a fortnight from spring to late
summer. In autumn apply a feed
that is high in phosphates and
potassium to encourage the
formation of next year's flowers.

Be aware! Satin wood is not an
easy subject for an indoor bonsai.
In addition to providing humidity
and good light, you will need to
check regularly for aphids and
greenhouse whitefly, which
often leave sticky honeydew
on the leaves, on which
sooty mould develops.
Aphids can be picked off
by hand. You should also
mist to clean the leaves and
apply a systemic insecticide if
any problem persists. Red spider
mites will be a problem if the
plants are not kept in a sufficiently
humid environment.

Murraya paniculata

Podocarpus macrophyllus

Chinese yew, kusamaki, Buddha pine

half-hardy • evergreen • easy to keep • interesting bark • red-purple berries

This species of podocarpus develops into a conical, rather upright tree with attractive red-brown bark. The leaves are dark green, lighter beneath, and held in upright shoots known as candles. Red-purple berries are borne on female plants in autumn. The plant is suitable for most bonsai styles except windswept and is widely available from bonsai nurseries. Two types of Chinese yew are used for indoor bonsai: the short-leaved *P. macrophyllus* 'Nivalis' and the longer-leaved *P. macrophyllus* 'Maki'.

Where to keep them

This species is native to China and Japan and It Is half-hardy In temperate areas (zone 7).

Above: The leaves of podocarpus resemble yew. This is *Podocarpus macrophyllus* 'Nivalis', the small-leaved variety.

Nevertheless, it prefers cool conditions, in both summer and winter. Keep Chinese yew In a bright position or partial shade in winter, at a temperature of 6–20°C (43–68°F), and stand outslde In summer In full sun.

How to look after them

Repotting: Repot this species every two or three years in late spring, taking care not to damage the roots, which are particularly sensitive. Use a fertile, moisture-retentive but free-draining compost consisting of one part loam, two parts leaf mould and one part sharp sand.

Pruning and pinching: Prune the growing tips at any time while the plant is in growth. Unlike yews, these plants will not regenerate from old wood, so take care of the bark when you cut. Use small, sharp clippers to cut out candles, which are too tough to pinch out with fingers. Take care that you do not cut through the needles, which will become discoloured and might lead to die-back.

Wiring: Chinese yews can be wired at any time of year. Wait for young stems to harden before wiring them and remove the wire after eight to ten weeks.

Watering: Keep this podocarpus well watered at all times so that the compost is moist all year round. Mist the foliage in summer or use a watering can with a rose to 'shower' the plant, which cleans and freshens the foliage.

Feeding: From spring until late summer you should apply a high-nitrogen fertilizer once a month. In early autumn give one application of a general fertilizer.

Be aware! Although the compost must be kept moist, these plants will react badly to being overwatered, which will cause the leaves to turn grey, wither and drop. The leaves attract woolly aphids, but these can be picked off by hand or controlled with a systemic insecticide.

Podocarpus macrophyllus 'Nivalis'

indoor bonsai

Punica granatum

Pomegranate

half-hardy • deciduous • orange flowers • pretty fruits • interesting trunks

Although the genus contains two species, only *Punica granatum*, the pomegranate, which produces the well-known fruit, is widely grown. It has narrow, glossy, bright green leaves, which are tinged with bronze or red when they first emerge, orange-red flowers and yellow-brown fruits. The dwarf form *P. granatum* var. *nana* is grown mainly for its beautiful orange-pink flowers and tiny fruit. In Japan cultivars with twisted, gnarled trunks are highly prized. The species is usually trained into the informal upright style and it is widely available from bonsai nurseries.

Where to keep them

This species is native to a wide area from southeast Europe to the Himalayas, and it is half-hardy in temperate areas (zone 7). If it is indoors in summer it should kept in a bright, sunny position, although plants should be moved outdoors to a position in full sun in summer if possible. Pomegranates will flower only if they are in full sun, and fruits will form in autumn only in temperatures of 13–16°C (55–61°F). In winter, when they have no leaves, the temperature can be as low as 3°C (37°F), and plants will even withstand 0°C (32°F) for short periods. Plants that are too warm in winter will develop weak, straggly shoots.

Above: The fruit of the dwarf pomegranate (*Punica granatum* 'Nana') set easily in summer and will remain on the plant until the following spring.

How to look after them

Repotting: Pomegranates should be repotted every three or four years. The best time is during early spring. Use a fertile, free-draining compost consisting of two parts loam and one part sharp sand.

Pruning and pinching: Prune the new shoots after flowering if they grow too long. Pinch out the growing tips to maintain the shape of the plant and stimulate the growth of new flowering shoots. Avoid pruning and pinching out these plants during summer, as this will remove the flowering buds from the tips of the shoots.

Punica granatum

Wiring: Branches can be wired from the end of spring until summer. Leave the wires in place for about one year.

Watering: Water pomegranates regularly in summer, making sure that the compost never dries out. In winter keep the compost just moist. Mist the leaves in summer.

Feeding: From early spring to summer apply a general fertilizer once a month. In late summer change to a low-nitrogen feed.

Be aware! Sap-sucking insects, such as scale insects, aphids and whitefly, can be a problem for this species. They can be picked off by hand or removed through the use of a systemic insecticide or by spraying as soon as they are noticed. The trunks of old plants rot easily, so never let moss grow around the base.

indoor bonsai

Sageretia thea

Sageretia, bird plum cherry

tender • semi-evergreen • easy to keep • attractive bark • black berries

This species, which is also known as *Sageretia theezans*, is widely used for bonsai. It has an upright habit, small, glossy leaves and small black berries. The greyish bark peels away in irregular patches to reveal lighter grey beneath. This is a great favourite with bonsai enthusiasts in China and is a popular indoor bonsai, which can be recommended for newcomers to the hobby. It is suitable for most styles, including the windswept style.

Where to keep them

This species is native to central and southern Asia and is tender in temperate areas (zone 8). When they are grown indoors, sagoretias need a bright, sunny, draught-free position and a minimum winter temperature of 12°C (54°F). In summer they can be moved outdoors and kept in full sun.

How to look after them

Repotting: Repot sageretias every two or three years in mid to late spring. Use a free-draining compost consisting of two parts loam, one part peat (or garden compost) and one part sharp sand.

Pruning and pinching: Sageretias have hard wood, which must be pruned carefully so that the bark is not accidentally damaged. In early spring, before the plant starts into growth, remove any damaged or misplaced branches. Regularly prune the new shoots that grow vigorously during the growing season, taking care not to

Above: The bark of sageretia peels and flakes as the trunk enlarges, resembling the bark of eugenia (see pages 162–163) and that of plane trees.

encourage inward growth when pruning. Use small, sharp clippers to keep the foliage in shape, as the tips of the shoots are too stiff for pinching out with fingers. Be careful not to cut through any of the leaves, as this will cause them to discolour and drop.

Wiring: There is rarely any need to wire sageretias because the shaping is achieved through pruning, but if branches need to be wired it can be applied at any time of the year to hardened shoots. Do not leave the wire in place for longer than one year.

Watering: Sageretias should be kept moist at all times. Water more frequently in summer than in winter, but never overwater and never let the compost dry out completely. Keep the compost just moist in winter. The leaves will benefit from being misted in summer, especially if plants are kept indoors.

Feeding: Start feeding sageretias with a general fertilizer in spring when the new leaves appear. Continue feeding once a month until early autumn.

Be aware! Sap-sucking insect pests, such as scale insects, aphids and whitefly, can be a problem. Treat with a systemic insecticide if there are too many to remove by hand. If mildew occurs, water carefully into the compost and improve the humidity around the plant by standing the pot in a tray of pebbles or gravel.

Sageretia thea

indoor bonsai

Schefflera aboricola

Octopus tree, umbrella tree

tender • evergreen • easy to keep • attractive foliage

This shrub, which in the wild can grow to 30 m (100 ft) high, is familiar to many as a houseplant, when it is more usually about 1 m (3 ft) tall. The bright green, palmate leaves, composed of between seven and sixteen leaflets, are borne on slender, flexible stalks. It is tolerant of a range of environments and is one of the easiest indoor bonsai to grow because it is a true houseplant. The informal upright and clump styles suit this bonsai best, and it is also very good for growing on rock. Vast numbers of schefflera bonsai are produced in Hawaii, but outside the United States the species is not often available as bonsai.

Where to keep them

These plants, which are native to southeast Asia, are tender (zones 9–10). Scheffleras are probably the only indoor bonsai that will tolerate low light levels, and they do best in good but indirect light. Keep them out of draughts and make sure that the winter temperature is 16–20°C (61–68°F). They can be taken outdoors in summer, but there is no need to do this because scheffleras are quite happy indoors all year round. The average living room offers an ideal environment.

How to look after them

Repotting: Repot scheffleras once every two or three years in early spring. Use a moisture-retentive but free-draining compost consisting of equal parts of loam, peat (or garden compost) and sharp sand. Keeping these plants slightly potbound keeps the leaves smaller, while frequent repotting will result in large leaves.

Pruning and pinching: Cut back branches by half in spring to encourage the production of dense foliage. During the growing season, maintain the shape of the plant and encourage the growth of laterals by pinching back the growing tips of new shoots once two or three leaves have formed.

Wiring: These plants are not wired. The shape of bonsai scheffleras is produced entirely through pruning.

Watering: Keep the compost slightly damp at all times, but do not overwater. Allow the surface of the compost to dry out a little before the next watering. Many

Above: The foliage of schefflera is very attractive. The leaves can be washed under a tepid shower occasionally to keep them free of dust.

of the scheffleras from Hawaii are grown over lava rock, which should be stood on a tray of gravel so that the roots can grow down into the gravel from where they will draw up water and nutrients. The leaves will benefit from occasional misting.

Feeding: Apply a liquid general fertilizer once a month from spring to late summer.

Be aware! Scheffleras are susceptible to scale insects and woolly aphids. If there are too many to remove by hand, apply a weak, systemic insecticide.

Schefflera aboricola

Serissa foetida

Serissa, tree of a thousand stars

tender • evergreen • challenging • star-shaped flowers • range of colours

This small evergreen shrub with wiry stems has delicate, glossy, dark green leaves, which emit an unpleasant scent (hence *foetida*) when they are crushed. It produces small, star-shaped white flowers throughout the summer. Variegated forms with cream-edged leaves have been developed, including 'Variegata' and 'Variegated Pink', which has pink flowers. The informal upright and cascade styles are most appropriate for this plant. Serissas are exported in vast numbers from China for sale in the West as indoor bonsai, but they are fairly difficult to keep and are not ideal 'starter' plants for a newcomer.

Where to keep them

Serissas are tender plants (zones 8–10) from southeast Asia, which need a bright, warm, humid position. Plants that are grown indoors in summer can be kept on a bright windowsill (although the average living room is not the ideal environment). In winter, when temperatures near the window fall or when curtains are drawn, they should be moved to a draught-free position with a temperature of 15–19°C (59–66°F). Although serissas will tolerate short periods at 7°C (45°F), the leaves will drop and branches will die back if they are left in the cold for too long. In summer, when temperatures are above 22°C (72°F), they can be moved outside and kept in full sun.

How to look after them

Repotting: Repot your serissa in early to mid spring only if the tree is growing strongly; otherwise, it is best to leave your plant well alone, because repotting can do more harm than good. Use a general compost consisting of equal parts of loam, peat (or garden compost) and sharp sand. These plants also grow well in a peat-based compost with some extra sharp sand added.

Pruning and pinching: Prune the shoot tips during the growing season to keep the plant in good shape, but be careful not to remove too many of these because the flowers are borne on the new growth. This plant is not pinched.

Above: The variegated form of serissa has very attractive foliage. A bright environment will encourage colourful leaves.

Wiring: Serissas take to wiring well, but be careful to wire only the woody branches. Do not wire branches that are still soft. The wire can be applied between early summer and early autumn, and the process repeated the following year if necessary. Don't leave the wires on for more than one year.

Watering: Keep the rootball moist at all times, watering more frequently in summer, when the plant is growing, than in autumn and winter. Use water that is at room temperature and allow the surface of the compost to dry slightly between waterings.

Serissa foetida

Feeding: Apply a general fertilizer every two or three weeks throughout the growing season, but stop feeding for a month in midsummer. Do not feed immediately after repotting.

Be aware! Serissas are temperamental plants, so do not be discouraged if your first bonsai dies. Scale insects can be a problem, and these plants are also susceptible to aphids. Spray with an appropriate insecticide at the first sign of infestation.

Ulmus parvifolia

Chinese elm

hardy • deciduous or semi-evergreen • easy to keep • versatile

This is undoubtedly the most common indoor bonsai sold in Europe and North America and is the best 'starter' plant for beginners. Millions are exported from China every year in all shapes, styles and sizes. (They are sometimes imported and sold as 'Zelkova' or *Zelkova sinensis* to get around import regulations, but they are different plants from true *Zelkova* (see pages 102–103.) Chinese elms are the easiest indoor species to grow and the most reliable; however, they should not be confused with the hardier forms, which have a rough bark (see pages 100–101). They are suitable for any bonsai style.

Where to keep them

Chinese elms like lots of light, so keep your plants in a bright position, such as a windowsill in your kitchen, bathroom or living room. Lack of light will result in pale, straggly shoots. They will do better in a cool room than a warm one. If you do not want to grow your Chinese elm as an indoor bonsai, it can be grown outdoors because these plants will tolerate wide temperature variations (zones 6–9). Plants that are grown indoors all year round will be semi-evergreen (or even evergreen), while outdoor specimens will lose their leaves in winter.

How to look after them

Repotting: Repot Chinese elms only when the tree is potbound and do not repot unnecessarily. This is best done in early spring, as the new leaves are about to emerge. Most commercial bonsai can be left in the original pot for at least two years from the time of purchase.

When you repot, use Akadama soil or a peat-based compost, consisting of two parts peat (or garden compost) and one part sharp sand.

Pruning and pinching: In early spring, prune Chinese elm to remove any unwanted branches.

The fine branches should be trimmed to thin them out as necessary, as indoor Chinese elms are prone to die-back if the twigs become too congested. Keep the plant looking neat by pinching out the growing tips of new shoots, as soon as two or three leaves emerge on the stem.

Above: The serrated leaves of the indoor Chinese elm are mid to dark green in colour. In the autumn, they turn yellow and fall.

Wiring: Wiring will not usually be necessary if you have bought a commercial bonsai, which will have been wired in the early stages of its training. In any case, most shaping is achieved through pruning. If you do need to wire a Chinese elm, do so between late spring and mid autumn. The wires can be left on for one year.

Watering: Keep the compost moist at all times, but do not overwater. It is better to wait until the surface of the compost has dried out a little between waterings. Plants need less water in winter than in summer. Chinese elms prefer fairly humid conditions, so stand the bonsai pot in a shallow tray filled with pebbles or gravel. Misting the plants occasionally will also be beneficial.

Feeding: Feed Chinese elms only between spring and autumn, when the plant is growing.

Be aware! When it is grown indoors, the Chinese elm is very susceptible to red spider mites, aphids and whitefly. Sudden loss of leaf is usually a sign of infestation, so spray with an appropriate insecticide. Standing the tree outside and spraying with a jet of water will dislodge many insects and do the tree no harm.

The foliage of indoor Chinese elms sometimes turns yellow and drops for no apparent reason. This is often caused by a change in the plant's environment – such as moving the tree from a cool to a warm room or moving it indoors from outside – so always take the time to allow the plants to acclimatize to new conditions.

Ulmus parvifolia

indoor bonsai

indoor bonsai

Zanthoxylum piperitum

Japan pepper

hardy • deciduous • easy to keep • attractive foliage • red berries

This tree is the source of Sichuan peppercorns. It has glossy, dark green, pinnate leaves, which turn yellow in autumn. In early summer greenish-yellow flowers appear, and these are followed by tiny red berries. The bark is aromatic. It is an attractive subject for indoor bonsai, and although it was introduced only recently to the West as a bonsai, it is becoming more popular as an easy-to-keep indoor subject. This plant is best grown in the informal upright style.

Where to keep them

The species comes originally from China, Korea, Japan and Taiwan, and it is hardy in temperate areas (zones 7–10), although as a bonsai it should be treated as an indoor plant. Keep it in a bright position, such as on a windowsill, but move it outdoors during summer and stand it in full sun.

How to look after them

Repotting: Repot Japan peppers every other year. The best time to repot is in mid spring just before the new leaves emerge. Use a free-draining, loam-based compost.

Pruning and pinching: Hard pruning is only necessary if you wish to restructure the branches. During the growing season, keep the tree looking trim by pruning back new growth and pinching out the growing tips when two to three sets of compound leaves have sprouted.

Wiring: *Zanthoxylum piperitum* has very stiff branches that are not suitable for conventional wiring. Hold the branches in place with guy wires (see page 197). Guy wires need to be left on for at least a year for the branches to set.

Watering: Make sure that your Japan pepper is well watered throughout the growing season. In winter keep the compost just moist.

Above: The small, glossy pinnate leaves of the Japan pepper are both attractive and highly aromatic, as is the bark.

Zanthoxylum piperitum

If the compost is allowed to dry out completely the plant will die. Misting is advisable if the room's atmosphere is very dry.

Feeding: Apply a high-nitrogen fertilizer in spring when the plant starts into growth. From summer until autumn, give a general fertilizer once a month.

Be aware! Aphids will cluster on new shoots. If the plant is standing outside, remove them by jetting them with water. Otherwise, pick them off by hand or apply an appropriate systemic insecticide. This is an extremely easy plant to grow.

looking
after
bonsai

Shaping, pruning and pinching

The shapes of most bonsai are artificial. Even bonsai collected from the wild, known as *yamadori* (a Japanese word meaning 'collected from the mountain'), require some shaping and wiring. There are two basic types of shaping: structural or creative, and refinement. Structural shaping is the initial hard pruning given to an untrained tree or shrub to create the structure of the future bonsai. Refinement shaping is carried out on bonsai that are already shaped in order to enhance their appearance. On-going light pruning and pinching are then required on a regular basis to keep your bonsai small and neat.

Tools

There are hundreds of different tools on the market for the bonsai hobbyist, ranging from twig- and branch-cutting implements to power tools for carving, and brushes for cleaning bark. For a beginner, all that is needed is a pair of ordinary garden secateurs or pruners, wire of different sizes, and a pair of pliers for cutting wire. Of the specialist bonsai tools, the most useful are the concave branch cutter, the twig-pruning scissors, the root-pruning scissors and the root hook or rake. Other bonsai tools are useful but not essential for most growers.

Structural shaping

Hard pruning is done to create a new bonsai or to reshape a tree that has lost its form. It is best done in spring or midsummer, when the tree is in growth and wounds will heal more easily.

There are some 21 bonsai styles or shapes, and different styles suit different trees: the weathered

driftwood style, for example, is better suited to the sturdy trunks of conifers than to delicate maples, whose slender trunks would work better as a forest group. Fortunately for the beginner, the basic shape of most bonsai is conical and simply trimming a tree

into a good conical form will create an attractive bonsai. Further refining it with wiring will make it look even better (see pages 196–197). It takes a trained eye to create a bonsai from an ordinary shrub; use pictures of good bonsai and tree shapes in nature as references.

Pruning branches

1 Use a concave branch cutter or a saw to remove large branches, cutting in as close as you can to the main trunk of the plant. The concave shape of this cutter ensures the remaining stub does not spoil the line of the trunk.

2 After removing a large branch of a non-resinous tree, seal the wound immediately with Japanese cut paste, available from bonsai stockists. Make sure all the edges are covered. The paste will fall off naturally as the wound heals.

Pruning

Branches and stems are lightly pruned to refine or maintain the appearance of the tree. Light pruning also helps to make your bonsai healthier, allowing light to penetrate the inner branches, improving air circulation and helping to keep pests and disease to a minimum.

A deciduous tree usually needs to be pruned twice a year in order to maintain its shape. Evergreen bonsai do not require trimming as often, because they are not usually as vigorous as deciduous trees. Avoid cutting through any leaves or needles when you are pruning, as this will turn the tips brown. Cut back to dormant buds to stimulate new shoots and the development of good branch ramification.

Pruning flowering subjects is always a compromise between maintaining the shape of the bonsai and taking care to ensure that there will be adequate supply of new buds for next year's flowers. The flowering buds are usually borne on the previous year's growth. If that is the case, pruning back too hard in summer will mean sacrificing the following year's crop of flowers. On the other hand, you shouldn't let new shoots extend too far, because this will spoil the shape of the tree and inhibit the development of laterals, the secondary shoots that actually carry the flowering buds.

From time to time, you may need to let the tree have a rest, leaving shoots to grow unchecked so that the bonsai regains vigour. This is particularly true of deciduous species. Fruiting and flowering trees should be allowed to rest once every three or four years.

Pinching

This is the term for removing the growing tip of a new shoot, using a pair of tweezers or the thumb and forefinger. It is done throughout the growing season to maintain the overall shape of the tree, and it must be carried out when the new shoots are still soft. The tips of deciduous trees are usually pinched out when two or three new leaves appear, and pines are also controlled by selective removal of the candles.

Fortunately, this chore is not as onerous as it sounds, because the shoots grow in spurts. In one year a tree will produce new shoots a limited number of times. Pines produce new candles only once a year, whereas other evergreens and deciduous bonsai do so two or three times a year.

Trees grown principally for their foliage can be pinched quite freely, but those grown for their flowers need more care. You don't want to be pinching off the flowering shoots that are usually borne on the tips of the new shoots. Thus on flowering subjects,

Above: Use the forefinger and thumb to pinch out pine candles as they elongate in late spring. Remove the strongest and leave one or two in each cluster to develop.

pruning and pinching is not usually done after midsummer when the flower buds for the following year will have set. You can recognise potential flower buds by their plumpness. If the buds at the leaf axils are not plump, then they will in all probability be leaf buds and not potential flower buds.

Leaf pruning

This is the total or partial defoliation of a deciduous bonsai, performed to introduce sunlight into the twig structure and to induce a new crop of leaves, which will usually (though not always) be smaller in size and will emerge after four or five weeks. Leaf pruning should only be done on healthy trees or on trees that have become dehydrated.

Wiring

The use of wire in bonsai is similar to the use of a brace for shaping children's teeth. By applying wire of the correct strength to a branch or trunk, the shape in which it is bent will set over a period of time. This modern way of styling bonsai is a convenient and quick method of achieving a desired shape. Before wiring was used, the ancient Chinese and Japanese practitioners created bonsai shapes by pruning and tying down the branches with bamboo sticks and weights.

Type of wire

The wires used for bonsai are specially annealed (softened) iron, aluminium and copper wires. They come in different gauges to cater for a wide range of branch and trunk thicknesses. For the amateur, aluminium wire is the easiest to handle. Copper is used by professionals for training coniferous bonsai, as the wire holds better and is less obtrusive.

However, it can be a bit stiff if you are not used to wiring. Different practitioners have their own preferences for wire types.

Judging the appropriate size of wire to use is largely common sense and comes with experience (you could practise on a twig first). If you use a gauge of wire that is too thin, then it won't be strong enough to do the job. If it is too thick, it could damage the branch.

The optimum size will depend on the pliability and thickness of the branch, so test the stiffness of the branches before you choose your wire. Bear in mind that you can use different thicknesses of wire on the same tree, as you move from thicker to thinner branches.

How to wire

Measure the branches you wish to wire and cut a piece of wire approximately 1½ times this length. You need to anchor the wire securely, by coiling it around the trunk or the parent branch, otherwise it will not be taut enough to bend the branch you wish to shape. Move along the branch from the anchored point, coiling the wire firmly and pulling the branch into the desired position. Take care not to trap either needles or leaves under the wire. Work gently to avoid cracking; you may need to wire in stages, tightening the wire after a couple of weeks to bend the branch further. Thick branches of coniferous trees can be wrapped with raffia to prevent

This illustration demonstrates good wiring, with the wire coiled at an angle of 45 degrees to the branch and the end of the wire anchored securely. Don't twist the wire too firmly or it will scar the tree.

In the 'one wire, two branches' method, a single piece of wire links two adjacent branches, so that one acts as the anchor for the other. This avoids having to wind the wire round the trunk.

them from snapping or breaking. How long to leave the wire on will depend on how thick and old the branch is. Young, vigorous shoots can set in as little as five to six months. Thicker branches may take two or more years to set.

If the wire is left on for too long it will leave a scar, although this is not necessarily detrimental as the healed marks can lend character to the tree, making it look gnarled and old. If you do not wish to mark the branch that is being wired, then you must remove or reposition the wire as soon as it starts to bite into the bark.

Keep an eye on the wires as the tree grows in summer; maples scar particularly easily. To prevent scarring when removing the wires, use angled wire cutters and avoid uncoiling it. If scarring does occur, seal the wound with cut paste.

Guy wires

If a branch is too thick to be wired into position in the conventional way (thick deciduous branches are more prone to snapping than coniferous and are therefore not often wired in the conventional way), or you don't want to mark the branch or disfigure, you can use a guy wire instead. Tie a strong piece of wire to a suitable point on the branch and secure it to the trunk or another strong branch below. There are some disadvantages to using guy wires: they tend to be unsightly and you cannot obtain twists and bends in the branch through this method.

Jins and sharis

Bonsai driftwood carvings, which seek to replicate the hollow trunks and deadwood found on trees in nature, have become very popular in recent years, especially in the West. The fashion has been stimulated by the great Japanese bonsai artist Masahiko Kimura, whose carved masterpieces are sculptures in their own right. Jin is the term for deadwood on a branch, while shari refers to a stripped trunk effect.

Jins and sharis can be made at any time of the year, although in the case of pines, avoid mid to late summer, when the sap is rising. With other species, summer is a better time to make driftwood, because any scars and cuts will heal over quickly. Cut paste should be applied to the edges of the bark to facilitate healing.

These effects look best on thick trunks and branches, as the wood reduces to nothing if attempted on thin trunks and branches. Manual tools such as chisels are seldom used now, but take great care when working with power tools. Protective gear such as face mask, safety helmet, gloves and gauntlets are absolutely essential and bystanders should be careful too.

Above: Some growers deliberately leave the shaping wires permanently embedded in the trunk or branch in order to make it swell and thicken.

Do not attempt to use power tools to shape your bonsai unless you have had proper training.

The authentic white bleached effect which is seen on some bonsai is achieved by applying lime sulphur or bleach to the dry dead wood. Once the driftwood effect has been created, the wood should in any case be preserved by applying lime sulphur to the wood once or twice a year when the weather is dry.

Watering and feeding

All plants need water and nutrients to grow. Like any container-grown plants, bonsai have to be watered regularly and they also need to be supplied with nutrients during the growing season. One of the commonest causes of death in bonsai is poor watering. Remember that small pots dry out much faster than large ones and will need watering more often. However, don't water too much – few trees will survive with their roots in waterlogged compost.

Watering outdoor bonsai

You should usually start to water outdoor bonsai when they start into growth in spring. This is when deciduous trees come into leaf and new shoots appear on evergreen trees. Continue to water throughout the growing season, which in temperate areas is from early to mid spring until early to mid autumn. If trees are outside in winter the moist air and rain is usually sufficient to keep them alive. However, if there has been no rain for several days, you will need to water, even in winter.

During the growing season water every day, or even twice a day if it is hot and dry. Deciduous bonsai in particular need copious watering at this time. It is best to water in the early evening if you are watering once a day, or morning and evening if you are watering twice a day.

Water with a garden hose (if you can) or with a watering can. For deciduous trees, especially those with delicate leaves such as the maples, it is worth fitting your hose or can with a fine rose head to avoid causing damage. Drench the soil thoroughly by applying water to the rootball for a full ten seconds – leave it to soak through for a few minutes and then repeat the whole process until the water drains through the drainage holes. Water the entire tree – the rootball, foliage, trunk, branches and all. Avoid watering in the midday sun or you will scorch the leaves. Instead, soak the rootball.

When you are watering flowering bonsai, take care that you do not splash droplets onto the petals, which are easily marked. Do not water flowering trees in full sun or the flowers and foliage will be scorched.

Above: Bonsai like this forest group need to be heavily drenched to ensure that all the trees receive sufficient water.

Watering indoor bonsai

Indoor bonsai must be watered throughout the year, although they will need more water in the growing season and less in the dormant period of autumn and winter. Some species require less water than others, and this is noted in the entries for specific trees. Do not let the compost dry out, but hold off watering if it feels already damp. Use a small watering can or a cup or glass. Some people water by soaking the entire pot in a bowl of water until the air bubbles stop coming out. This is fine, but not a convenient method if the bonsai is large and heavy.

If the bonsai become dusty, take them to the shower and use tepid water to wash off the dust. In warm weather, take them outside and use a hose or watering can.

Indoor bonsai should be stood in a shallow tray containing gravel or pebbles so that excess water drains from the compost and collects in the tray. The water that collects in the drip tray helps to keep the bonsai moist and creates a humid atmosphere around the tree. Never stand indoor bonsai permanently in a deep bowl of water because this can rot the roots. A plant's roots have to take up oxygen from the soil around them, and if the soil is waterlogged the bonsai will eventually 'drown'.

Misting, or creating a fine spray of water particles using a hand sprayer, is done to increase

Above: Fertilizer can be supplied either in solid or liquid form. Be careful to give the right amount as overfeeding can be just as harmful as underfeeding.

humidity. Misting is advisable for indoor bonsai if the room is very dry, but should never be done as a substitute for watering. Misting an indoor tree with a hand sprayer is not enough to water the tree.

Feeding

Even more than other container-grown plants, bonsai have to be given nutrients at regular intervals because of the limited volume of soil in which they grow. With most bonsai, fertilizer should be applied only during the growing season. If they are given nutrients when they are not growing, the fertilizer will be wasted or it will encourage growth at the wrong time of year and cause stress to the tree. Plants need a range of minerals and

trace elements, especially nitrogen (N), which promotes leaf growth; phosphorous (P), which encourages root development; and potassium (K), which enables plants to produce flowers and fruit. Artificial fertilizers are usually labelled to show the ratio of N:P:K elements that they contain and you should choose different formulations for different times of the year (see the individual tree entries for specific instructions). A low-nitrogen fertilizer will be high in phosphorous and potassium, which is why it is often used to encourage flower and fruit formation. Rose fertilizer is good for this purpose. Artificial fertilizers usually also contain the other elements, such as calcium, that plants need.

Environment

If your tree is ailing, it may be that you are keeping it in the wrong environment. Indoor bonsai can be put outdoors only in summer, and even outdoor bonsai need protection from extremes of heat and cold. Too little light and your plant will not thrive; too much sun and the leaves will scorch. Compost is also vital: it should have enough body to support the tree and must be free draining, so the roots can breathe.

Temperature and light

If you have only a few outdoor bonsai, keeping them near the wall of the house may be sufficient protection from sun and cold. An unheated greenhouse is protection in winter, and an unheated shed can be used for brief periods, but is too poorly lit for the long term.

Indoor bonsai are usually tropical or subtropical. The best position for plants is a windowsill with maximum light. They also need a constant temperature. Some enthusiasts rig up special grow lamps, heaters and humidifiers, but this is unnecessary if you only have a few trees. As soon as the spring frosts have passed, put your indoor bonsai outdoors, so that they can get sunshine, rain and fresh air. Move them indoors in autumn.

Compost

Many Japanese growers use Akadama soil, consisting of red clay granules which create a moisture-retentive but free-draining growing medium. It is available outside Japan, and although it is expensive, many enthusiasts prefer to use it. Avoid 'bonsai compost' from non-specialist nurseries as this is usually just peat-based compost.

You can also make your own growing medium by mixing equal quantities of peat, sharp sand and loam. Finely chopped bark or garden compost are good substitutes for peat. The proportion of the three basic ingredients should vary depending on the species. Pines and junipers prefer an open, sandy mixture, and you could use two parts sharp sand, one part peat and one part loam for these species. Fruiting and flowering trees usually prefer a loamier soil, with up to 50 per cent loam. Include as much as 50–75 per cent peat (or peat substitute) for indoor bonsai.

Above: A shelter made of corrugated plastic sheeting is ideal for protecting your bonsai in winter.

Repotting

Bonsai should be repotted only when they are potbound – that is, when the roots completely fill the pot. It is a misconception that they require frequent repotting and root trimming to keep them small. Frequency of repotting depends on how vigorous the species is (see individual plant entries for more details), on the warmth of the climate and on the tree's age. As a very general rule, bonsai less than 15 years old should be repotted every two to three years, while older trees need repotting every four to five years.

Time of year

Check whether your bonsai need repotting in early spring. This is the best time for repotting: the trees are about to start into growth, and any cuts made to the roots will heal quickly and new roots will soon grow. It can be harmful to repot at other times, and you should never repot a deciduous tree when it is in full leaf – that is, during the growing season – because cutting its roots will make it wilt. Conifers may not suffer to the same extent, but even these species should be repotted in spring. Should your pot break in the middle of the growing season – if it is blown over or accidentally knocked over – you should simply put it into a larger pot and wait until the following spring to repot it. Repot indoor bonsai in late spring, as early spring is too cold for disturbing the roots of indoor subjects.

How to do it

If you have established that the tree is potbound, begin by taking it out of its pot and teasing out the

Above: This bonsai is clearly very potbound. When the roots reach this condition, it is definitely time to repot the plant.

rootball with a rake or chopstick. Remove about one-third of the old compost from the rootball and cut off the long roots with a pair of scissors. This will make room for new compost to be introduced into the pot. Finally, replace the tree in

its container and insert fresh compost. Trees that are clearly sick or in poor health should not be repotted, as cutting the roots will do more harm than good. Seek advice from a reputable bonsai nursery if in doubt.

looking after bonsai

Propagation

Propagating trees for bonsai is just as easy as propagating trees for the garden. It is an enthralling and satisfying pastime and well worth the effort. There are three main methods: from seeds, cuttings, and by layering. You can also extend your collection by using mature nursery trees or trees dug up from the wild or your own garden. Experimenting with the different methods can be great fun.

Seeds

Use seeds and cuttings if you want to start growing small bonsai from scratch. There is no such thing as special bonsai seed. The seeds you use will grow eventually into large shrubs or trees – it is the pruning and shaping that makes a tree into a bonsai. Always use fresh seed, bought from a reputable supplier. Most species should be sown in autumn and left outside or in a cold frame to break the dormancy.

Use a seed compost or good-quality multi-purpose compost. When the seeds germinate in spring, prick out the seedlings when the first leaves have formed. Pot them into individual pots and let them grow on for at least one year before training. Conifers such as pines and junipers, and deciduous species such as *Acer* (maple), grow easily from seed.

Cuttings

Not all trees can be propagated from cuttings, but junipers, cryptomeria and *Chamaecyparis obtusa* (Hinoki cypress) do strike easily. Pines and larches do not grow well from cuttings. Among deciduous species, *Acer* and *Ulmus* (elm) are perhaps the easiest, while *Prunus* and beech are difficult.

Take cuttings no thicker than a matchstick, using sharp and sterile tools. Greenwood cuttings from the soft tips of shoots are taken in early summer. Ripe wood cuttings

Left: Japanese maple seedlings grow easily from collected seed.

Above: A heel cutting is a shoot attached to a 'heel' of the previous year's wood. For maples, these are more successful than nodal cuttings severed below an internode.

of evergreen shrubs are taken in late summer or early autumn, and hardwood cuttings from deciduous trees and shrubs are taken in late autumn or early winter.

Hormone rooting powder or liquid can speed up the process but is not essential. Use a medium of peat and sharp sand in equal parts. Some cuttings will strike in pure peat or even in pure sharp sand. Try different composts to see what works best.

Layering

This ancient method, still practised throughout Asia, involves restricting the flow of sap to a branch by removing a ring of bark or tying wire round it. The area is then wrapped in soil or moss and encased in a plastic bag to hold in moisture. Within a few weeks or months, roots will emerge. When sufficient have formed, the branch can be severed to grow as a tree. The method quickly produces mature plants. It is used for propagating maples, hornbeams, beech, willow, tamarix, crab apple, junipers, cypresses and larch. Some species, such as pine and oak, are not layered.

Nursery stock

You can create bonsai from mature nursery trees and save yourself years of waiting. Most bonsai enthusiasts use this quick and convenient method. Choose trees that have an interesting trunk and branches. Select the trunk line and visualize the shape of the bonsai you want to create. Once you have the image of the bonsai in your mind, it is simply a matter of pruning and wiring to achieve the end result.

Starter/field-grown material

Some nurseries sell plants of different ages that have been specially grown for bonsai. A good bonsai nursery will have trees that have already undergone some training, taking a lot of the drudgery out of the creative process. Characterful old specimens are not cheap, however; prices reflect the amount of work and time spent on each tree. Starter plants are popular with bonsai enthusiasts who like to express their creativity through this medium.

Collected material

Once you understand how to make bonsai, you can obtain the raw material from many different sources. You can get your plants, shrubs and trees from nurseries or from your own or friends' gardens. There is also a tradition among bonsai enthusiasts of collecting from the 'wild' – from forests, mountains and other open spaces – and although some people still do this, taking plants from the wild should not be encouraged and in some circumstances is illegal.

Problems

If you begin by choosing the right species and getting the best advice, you will have a head start with your bonsai. But sometimes, even if you lavish all possible care on them and do everything that is recommended, they still succumb to pests and diseases that are beyond your control. Following is a brief guide to identifying and dealing with some of the more common problems encountered with bonsai. Avoid excessive use of fertilizers or chemical sprays as this can be as great a cause of death as the pests and diseases themselves.

Yellowing leaves/excessive leaf drop

Yellowing of the leaves and excessive leaf drop can be the result of inadequate light, too much or too little water, or pest infestation. Some plants also react badly to being moved from one environment to another, so always allow your plants time to become acclimatized to new conditions. It can also be caused by chlorosis, a condition in which an inability to take up minerals from the soil results from factors such as low temperatures and waterlogging.

Pests

Insect pests can cause a lot of damage. Some of the sap-sucking insects weaken plants, distort shoots or transmit diseases from plant to plant. Other insects, such as vine weevils, attack the plants' roots and can cause fatal damage.

Aphids: Sap-sucking green, yellow, pink, black or white insects are often found on young shoots in spring. Small infestations can be removed by hand, and when plants are standing outside jetting water at the plant will dislodge the pests. There are several appropriate organic insecticides, including pyrethrum, derris and specialized soaps. Pirimicarb does not harm other, beneficial insects.

Red spider mite: If foliage becomes mottled and yellow-brown in midsummer and then the

Above: Yellowing leaves can simply indicate the onset of winter, rather than pest infestation or any other problem.

Above: Aphids are always a problem in early spring. They can do a lot of damage to the new leaves.

leaves drop from the plant, red spider mites are the probable culprits. These are minute, yellow-green mites, which crawl on fine silk webbing on the undersides of leaves. *Picea* (spruce) are often badly affected, but junipers and cedars are also susceptible. Increase humidity around plants and, if necessary, spray with malathion or bifenthrin, repeating the treatment if necessary.

Adelgids: These affect all pine species and larch. They resemble the white woolly aphids which host on certain plants such as beech and crassulas, but are easy to identify as they only affect the pines and larches. Adelgids are active from the early spring and if left untreated will multiply profusely and cause serious damage to the needles and young shoots. Most insecticides will kill this pest.

Vine weevils: In recent years vine weevils have become a major scourge of all container-grown plants. The adult weevils eat notches from the edges of leaves, but the main damage is done by the cream-coloured, C-shaped, legless larvae, which live in compost and eat a plant's roots. This either slows down growth or, if unchecked, kills the plant altogether. When you are repotting, search the compost for the larvae and kill any you find. Insecticides available to amateur gardeners are not reliable against this pest, and the best control is to water pathogenic nematodes, *Heterorhabditis megidis* or *Steinernema carpocapsae*, into the compost in late spring.

Scale insects: These sap-sucking insects are protected by white or greyish, waxy shells. They are often specific to particular genera – juniper scale and beech bark scale, for example. These insects are most vulnerable to insecticides, especially malathion, early in the year, before the newly hatched nymphs have developed their protective waxy covers.

Diseases

As long as you have started with healthy plants and keep them in optimum conditions you are unlikely to be troubled by diseases, but a few problems, such as mildew, can be persistent.

Mildew: This is a fungal problem, which takes the form of a white, powdery growth on leaf surfaces. If unchecked, it will spread to stems and even the entire plant. Some plants are bred to show some resistance. Take great care when watering not to splash the leaves but to direct the water to the compost. Remove and burn all infected leaves as soon as you notice them and, if necessary, spray with a suitable fungicide.

Fireblight: Members of the Rosaceae family are susceptible to this serious bacterial disease. Flowers die first, then leaves, then shoots. It occurs most frequently in periods of warm, wet weather, and the bacteria can be carried on tools or on raindrops. Remove and burn all infected plant material and disinfect all your tools that have come into contact with the plant.

Peach leaf curl: New leaves look puckered and blistered in spring and a layer of white spores appears on the leaf surface. The leaves drop but are usually followed by a second flush of leaves. If the disease is untreated, the tree's vigour will be impaired. Pick off and burn affected leaves, and prevent the problem arising by keeping the tree under cover in spring so that the spores cannot reach the tree. A winter spray of copper fungicide will help.

Galls: These are growths on leaves and stems and are caused by bacteria. They are unsightly, but they do not threaten the life of the plant. Oaks, rhododendrons (including Satsuki azaleas) and peaches tend to suffer from them. Simply remove the affected leaves and stems and burn them.

Above: Oak leaf gall will not harm your bonsai, but it looks extremely unsightly.

looking after bonsai

Author acknowledgements

One of the great joys of working as a bonsai professional is to communicate my knowledge through my talks and books. I have now written six books on bonsai and one on Japanese gardening, and I still get asked to write new titles. The feedback that I have received from readers all over the world has been most gratifying and I feel privileged to be able to share my knowledge with such a wide audience over a long period of time. None of this would have been possible without the encouragement of my wife Dawn who, despite her illness from breast cancer for over sixteen years, has been a constant source of inspiration. I am also indebted to my Indian bonsai friends, in particular Mr and Mrs Shri Dhar, for sharing their knowledge of tropical species. This book is dedicated to bonsai enthusiasts the world over, since bonsai is truly international now.

Photographic acknowledgements

All photographs copyright © Peter Chan except the following: pages 75 and 129 Dan Barton; page 93 David Johnson; page 97 Mauro Stemberger; page 171 John Trott.

Bonsai

All bonsai by Peter Chan except the following: pages 4 and 12 Terry Foster; pages 6, 35, 75 and 129 Dan Barton; pages 21, 153, 161, 165, 167, 177 and 185 Prabha Shri Dhar; page 93 David Johnson; page 97 Mauro Stemberger; page 145 Beryl Thorpe.

Publisher acknowledgements

Executive editor: Sarah Ford
Project editor: Fiona Robertson
Executive art editor: Tim Pattinson
Designer: Ginny Zeal
Senior production controller: Martin Croshaw